NAGA CULTURAL ATTIRES
AND
MUSICAL INSTRUMENTS

CASTES AND TRIBES OF INDIA-SERIES

1. Continuity and Change Among the Ahom/ **Nitul Kumar Gogai**
2. Ethnography of a Nomadic Tribe: A Study of Yanadi/ **N. Sudhakar Rao**
3. Mythos and Logos of the Warlis: A Tribal World View/ **Ajay Dandekar (Ed.)**
4. Naga Cultural Attires and Musical Instruments/ **A. Lanu Ao (Ed.)**
5. Socio-Cultural Study of Scheduled Tribes: The Pardhans of Maharashtra/ **S.R. Murkute**
6. The Banjara/ **S.G. Deogaonkar** and **Shailaja S. Deogaonkar**
7. The Kolam Tribals/ **S.G. Deogaonkar** and **Leena Deogaonkar Baxi**
8. The Korku Tribals/ **S.G. Deogaonkar** and **Shailaja S. Deogaonkar**
9. Tribal Dance and Songs/ **S.G. Deogaonkar** and **Shailaja S. Deogaonkar**

About the Author

An explorer of Naga Traditional Culture, Late Kajen Mongro belongs to Longkhum Village, son of Late Kikachiba and Late Nungsanglemla, born on 27th April, 1930 in his native village. Late Kajen Mongro retained the descendant's name of *Mongro*, his clan's identity. His father was a talented singer from whom he learned the folk songs and playing of all sort of traditional musical instruments. His father was once a Village Priest, the post exclusively reserved for Yar-Mongro clan; recalling the two prominent migration leaders, Mongrochang and Yarangchang.

After early schooling at Longkhum village, Late Kajen Mongro matriculated from Govt. High School, Mokokchung in 1956; passed Intermediate Arts (I.A) from St. Anthony's College, Shillong, in 1958, graduating later from Fazl Ali College, Mokokchung in 1965, and took his B.Ed. still later from Nagaland College of Education in 1980. After his graduation he served as Head Master in his native village for several years. Then after, he worked as Head Master of Sabangya Govt. M.E. School from 1965-69. His later assignments were, Assistant Teacher at Govt. High School Mokokchung, 1970-77, Sub-Inspector of Adult Education, Wokha, 1977-79; Inspector of Adult Education, 1981-84 and Cultural Officer Academy of Music and Dance, Kohima Nagaland under the Directorate of Arts and Culture from 26th December, 1984 and retired in 1994.

As a poet and promoter of Naga Culture, Late Kajen Mongro has published his first book, entitled 'AOR NARO KEN' (The Flower Songs of the Aos) in 1987, detailing the indigenous flowers of Nagaland enriching the flower culture of the people. Late Kajen Mongro got married with Nangshimongla Soya, daughter of Mr. & Mrs. Tsuknungmeren of Longkhum village in 1962. Leaving his dearest wife, two sons and four daughters, Kajen Mongro passed away on 14.3.96. at the age of 66 years and his body was buried in his native village Longkhum on 15.3.96.

Castes and Tribes of India Series-5

NAGA CULTURAL ATTIRES AND MUSICAL INSTRUMENTS

Written by
KAJEN MONGRO

Edited by
A. LANU AO

CONCEPT PUBLISHING COMPANY PVT. LTD.
NEW DELHI-110059

ISBN: 978-81-7022-793-9

First Published 1999

Published and Printed by

Concept Since 1974

Concept Publishing Company Pvt. Ltd.
A/15-16, Commercial Block, Mohan Garden,
New Delhi-110059 (India)
T: 91-11-41101460
E: publishing@conceptpub.com, *W*: www.conceptpub.com

DEDICATED

TO

MY BELOVED PARENTS

PREFACE

Late Kajen Mongro's next attempt was to publish this book after retirement from active service in 1994. But due to his ill health, this book could not be published when he was still alive.

Right from his boyhood, Late Kajen Mongro was a lover of songs, dance, art and festivals. He was a talented person in the field of Naga Culture. As a Master-Trainer of Culture and Art, Late Kajen Mongro was a man of wisdom. His contribution in the field of Naga Art and Culture is very significant and recordable. His book entitled, *Aor Naro Ken*, (The Flower Songs of the Aos) is one of the living examples which he published in 1987. He was a modeller of Naga Culture and worked for the cause of preserving and promoting it till his last breath.

Throughout his career, he was practicing his native culture which he loved most. He had collected huge amount of information on Naga Culture pertaining to various tribes. It was an additional privilege for him to join in the Department of Arts and Culture, Government of Nagaland, which he earned to serve as a Cultural Officer in the Academy of Music and Dance since 1984 till his retirement in 1994. He had attended in many occasions of Art and Culture Programmes at different levels and collected invaluable materials. He gained more knowledge by attending seminars, workshops, group discussions, trainings and cultural exposure activities both inside and outside the State of Nagaland. This book is, thus, the outcome of such experiences and his special interest towards the promotion and preservation of Naga culture through such documentation works. Because of these, he earned immense appreciation in the field of Fine Arts and Culture. He left behind us many lessons to be learned by the youngsters through this documentation work. Late Kajen Mongro was a practical man and lived a modest life.

In the later stage of his career; he became a researcher in the field of Anthropology and Sociology. This book itself tells us what kind of man he was. It brings back Kajen Mongro to our presence once again and keeps him alive forever through this book of wisdom.

It was on July 7th, 1995 when my wife and children met Kajen Mongro and his wife at Dimapur taxi stand incidentally. All of them wanted to go to Medziphema by taxi early. When my wife engaged a taxi, Mongro's family also came and boarded in the same taxi. However, he failed to recognise my wife and children totally. My wife was knowing him but she did not disclose her identity to him at that moment. While travelling together by taxi, he was sharing the sweetness of teaching profession with my wife; because he was also a teacher; and they were working together some years back. He and his wife were going to Medziphema to meet me but he could not identify my wife till that time. They all proceeded towards Medziphema in the same taxi. My wife and children were patiently hearing when Late Kajen Mongro was talking about Dr. Lanu on the way to my residence on that day. Late Mongro asked my wife:

> "Sister, where are you going and where will you get down"? "I am going to Medziphema Nagaland University Campus and get down there" she said "Oh! O-O, I am also going to Medziphema and shall get down there, because I am going to meet Dr. Lanu for a very important matter to be discussed with him", he said to my wife. She then jokingly said, "we are going to the same destination and the same house. I am Mrs. Dr. Lanu".

Filled with great joy and surprise he shooked hand with my wife and reached my house safely. This was the first attempt of Late Kajen Mongro, coming to my place to discuss about this book with me.

After a while, he sent me the manuscript of this book in a very raw form requesting me to do the editorial work on his behalf. While in Vellore Hospital, he wrote to me twice inquiring about the progress of this work. The first checking and improvement of the manuscript was then completed when he was still alive and sent back to him. After a while, his health became more critical and he passed away without seeing his book coming out in this form.

After his death in 1996, the same manuscript was again brought to me and further improvement was made thereafter in 1997 itself. I feel that this book would have been published much earlier and better than this if Late Kajen Mongro survived to live atleast a few more years with us. His last word to me was:

The Author Mr. Kajen Mongro

Mrs. and Mr. Kajen Mongro

> "Dear brother Lanu I don't like to die before completing this book. I will be the happiest person to die if this book is published when I am still alive. My health is uncertain now, and I may leave this temporal world soon to live with God forever more in Heaven"

Soon after, he passed away before the publication of this book. I wish that Late Jaken Mongro sees this book coming out in this form.

Now, this book is published in his memory as a *Posthumous Work* and presented in three broad chapters. In the first chapter, 19 different items of men's dresses are discussed. These are mainly worn during festival and important occasions. The Nagas are colourful and attractive hill people. They look more grand and beautiful when they are in complete traditional dresses and ornaments. This chapter describes about various ornamental items and also the process of making based on traditional practical experiences. The various names of ornaments called by different tribes, their meanings, utility and their social functions are clearly discussed in this chapter.

In the second chapter, the women's dresses worn by various Naga women are discussed covering nine major items of such attires selected for this purpose. Naga women are playing significant roles in contemporary society. The distinctive women attire of different Naga tribes makes their culture more beautiful which is liked by many people of the world today. This chapter gives a detailed account of women's attire.

The last and the third chapter is an account of Naga musical instruments. The Nagas are music lovers. Different types of musical instrument used by the Nagas are explained in this chapter. Every musical instrument has its own utility and functions. The meaning of the sounds and their societal control measures through such traditional musical instrument are recorded in this chapter.

With due acknowledgement, we wish to give thanks to all the tribal leaders and friends of different Naga tribes who have supplied the required information and helped us for successful publication of this book whose names are too many to be recorded here. It was Prof. N. Pandey, Department of Geology and Dr. Sachdeva of Linguistics, Nagaland University who have contributed their invaluable thoughts and encouraged for early publication of this book: we are thankful to them. It was Mr. Imkongtoshi, Stenographer, Nagaland University, who typed out this manuscript sincerely within a very short time for which we are thankful to him. Above all, we are deeply indebted to

S.C. Jamir, Chief Minister of Nagaland for his financial assistance, given to the author as a sign of encouragement to the local writer. I remain grateful to Mr. Ashok Kumar Mittal, the Concept Publishing Company, New Delhi who has taken up this publication work with keen interest. I am grateful to him too.

Needless to say that there may be errors or omission and commission. I am aware of that. It will be a great help to me if the readers take trouble to point them out with constructive suggestion for further improvement of this book in future.

A. LANUNUNGSANG AO
Prof. & Head
Department of Sociology
Nagaland University
Headquarters, Lumami.
P.O. Mokokchung
Post Box No. 12

CONTENTS

1

THE MEN'S ATTIRE

1.1 The Hornbill Feather

The earth is full of different birds with different colours of different sizes among which hornbill is a very significant bird. This bird can be found in many parts of the world though its existence is badly threatened due to ecological destruction around the world. It has many endearing qualities of which the most attractive part is the tail, which is marked with strip of a black and white spreading at regular intervals. The Creator has made this bird so distinctly not only with beautiful tails and head but with other qualities like the voice of a tiger which is known as *Tenem Nganger* in Ao. which means hornbill's voice resembles with that of a sound of a tiger in anger.

By nature, hornbill never stays in ordinary forest except in the deep forest full of gigantic trees. It makes its nest mainly in the tall and big trees. Normally, the nest of the hornbill can be found only in the holes of such big trees. The holes are inter-connected both inlet and outlet. The young ones are hatched out in such nest inside the holes. During hatching period, inlet and outlet are closed with mud leaving a small hole till the young ones could fly off. Through this small hole the male hornbill use to feed them regularly. During the breeding period, the female is kept in a tree hole. The mother hornbill sheds all its feathers during hatching period, after which it grows a little later along with its babies. Throughout hatching and feeding period only the male takes the entire responsibility of feeding the young ones and mother. So, whenever a hunter shoots a male hornbill during the feeding season, the mother and the babies die out of starvation. Therefore, it is highly restricted not to kill the male hornbill during this period as per Naga customs. There is a popular belief that the "hornbill sounds like tiger because they are fed by the remnant of tiger's prey". As the young ones become older, the mother use to train them to jump from one branch to another branch of the trees. This is the beginning of socialisation in the family of this bird just like human society. Thus, a hornbill family is considered as the family of human being in a form of its socialisation.

It is interesting to understand how this bird is caught in Naga society. The trick to catch this bird in the dense forest is a difficult task for a hunter. Some people climb up even to the tallest tree by making ladder from one tree to another tree to reach the top of the tree where the bird sits and eats fruits has to volunteer a lot. Such a man is called *Nakyur*, the tree climber like a monkey climbs even though there is another way like bridge or, a ladder and he has to climb up with all the difficulties and tactics to catch the bird and there he puts the Ngepen/ Angi (a kind of comb made of rubber) on the branches of the tree where the hornbill may sit and eat food. After laying all the possible traps on the branches, he comes down from the tree. This job has to be done before dawn break. Thereafter, the hunter will be watching the coming of hornbill. Just after the sunrise, the bird wants to fly in and is caught in the trap. If he is lucky enough he may catch a few in number. The easiest method of catching this bird is the use of bow and arrow. Many Nagas use this bow especially by the people of Tuensang district of Nagaland. After the bird is caught, the hunter collects the feathers with great joy either for his personal use or for sale. Its tail part of the feathers is more expensive and costly. By tradition, one feather especially the tail part was considered equivalent to a Mithun's head. That is why, a hornbill feather was meant for the rich man who could give Mithun sacrifice to the villagers and for those of the warriors. The bird's hunter thus sells out its feathers with higher price to his fellow friends.

In the past, only those persons who were warriors and rich men were allowed to put it. Nobody could put it unless and until he becomes a warrior or a rich man. Today, many people put feathers in their coronet while dancing without any restriction. The Aos are fond of using this feather in the headgear during the time of festival dances, like *Moatsu* and *Tsungrem Mong*. The headgear is known as "*Temkhu*" in Ao dialect.

Among the Rengmas, hornbill feathers are used during dancing and other festive occasions. This norm is same as that of the Aos to use this feather. They call their headgear *'Atamuku'* and the feather is known as *'Aghanuo'*. Among the Lothas 'Tukhu Emong' which falls on the 7th November is an occasion for such display of tribal finery, where the only renowned warriors for their valour are allowed to use their headgear with hornbill feathers. In Lotha dialect, this is called *'Emben'*.

The Semas also regard the hornbill feathers with great esteem and no festival would be completed without this finery display with this colourful headgear. In Sema dialect, it is called *'Aghachompi'* and this is proudly displayed during the *Tuluni* festival only by those men who have earned the merit to do so. The people who are highly honoured constitutes a very small group which includes only the rich and warriors who have excelled themselves. The Semas called the feather *'Aghachu'*. The same procedure is followed by the Sangtam tribe also. The *Aomongmong* is considered to be the biggest festival where they display these feathers with much pride. They called it *'Uzakhyu'*.

The people of Mon district generally use the country made gun and bow. They kill hornbill with such weapons. They put the hornbill feathers in their headgear mainly during the *Aoling Mongyu* festival. Also the Phom tribe display their dresses during their festival dances, and at that time they use this feather on their headgear, *Aoling Mongyu* is the biggest national festival of the Konyak tribe. In the month of July, the Chang tribe of Tuensang district use to observe their famous festival. In this festival dances, both men and women participate with great enthusiasm. Their famous and biggest festival it called *'Naknylam'*. In this festival, they wear particular headgear known as *Heiloikhon* and over it the dancer put hornbill feathers. Mitemnew is the national festival of Yimchunger and they too put hornbill feathers on their headgear. The Khiamungan tribe has got two important festivals, one is in April and the other is in the month of October. These two festivals are called '*Miu* and *Tsokum*' respectively. During these festivals, dancers do put hornbill feathers in their headgear.

Among the Angami tribe, 'Sekrenyie' is the biggest and sweetest festival of the year. Both men and women take part in dancing during this festive occasion. Young boys and girls do enjoy this festival with greatest joy and happiness. From times immemorial they put hornbill feathers in the headgear and they also keep a bundle of hairs on the head where feathers are put. It gives them a very beautiful and attractive look. They called it '*Thuvu Mia*'. The Chakhesang also have got their favourite national festival called 'Tsukhenyie'. During the observation of this occasion both men and women take part in dancing. Their headgear is most similar to that of the Semas, the Aos, the Rengmas etc; and they call it *'Piphu'*. As with other tribal dances, they decorate with hornbill feathers which is known as *'Theroma'* in their dialect. This feather is mostly worn by the male members. The Zeliang tribe do observe a festival which is called 'Nga-Ngai'. It is observed in the month of December during the winter season. Both men and women are involved in dancing during this festival. The Zeliang people are good dancers as in the case of other Naga tribals. In such a performance, they hold this feather in their hands. It provides a beautiful spectacle to the spectators. This feather is called '*Aguimia*' in Zeliang dialect. Today, the hornbill feather has become as one of the most common item of dresses used during every occasion of all Naga tribal festivals. The only problem is that the original feathers are not available because the population of this bird has already reduced to a great extent due to destruction of forest. This bird is now considered as an endangered bird from extinction.

1.2 The Coronet

For making the coronet, a slit cane is made circular by joining both the ends and tinge them up by cotton or woollen thread in such a way that the circumference of the round cane exactly fits the users' head. To make it more attractive, the backside of the circular cane is covered with white cotton. After making the proper joint, the bear's hair is pasted with the help of '*Konem*' a type of local adhesive and tied up on the cane strip from the end to the other. The hairs are then trimmed uniformly by *dao* in such a way that the front side of the coronet has little longer hair than the backside. Such type of coronet is known as *Temkhu* the traditional head-dress of the Ao Nagas. The coronet is further decorated by putting hornbill feathers on it in order to signify the status of outstanding personalities in the society such as richness, and bravity. The number of the hornbill feathers normally represents the number of human heads hunted and also the mithuns sacrificial feast offered to the villagers. In order to make more attractive, some people used to put the ripe red chillies on the top of their coronet.

Most of the Naga tribes, such as Aos, the Semas, the Lothas, the Angamis, the Rengmas, the Chakhesangs etc. use the coronet in all the special occasions putting hornbill feathers. These special feathers are considered as a symbol of honour, richness, warrior and other social status in Naga society. Those who are entitled to use such feathers take it as a pride while dancing during their respective festivals. In Ao society, a rich man's wife is also entitled to put hornbill feather on her

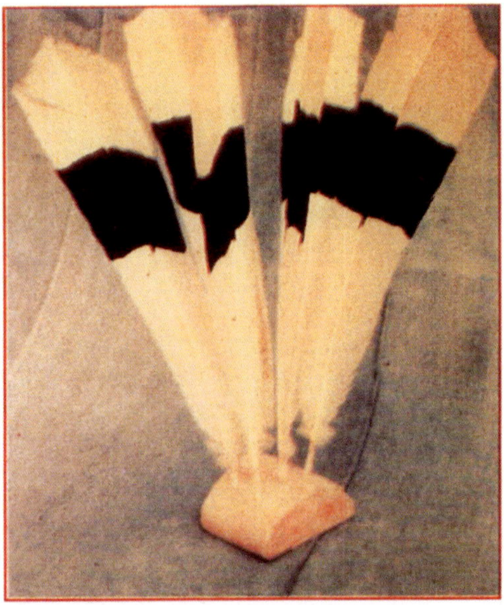

Fig. 1.1 : The Hornbill Feather

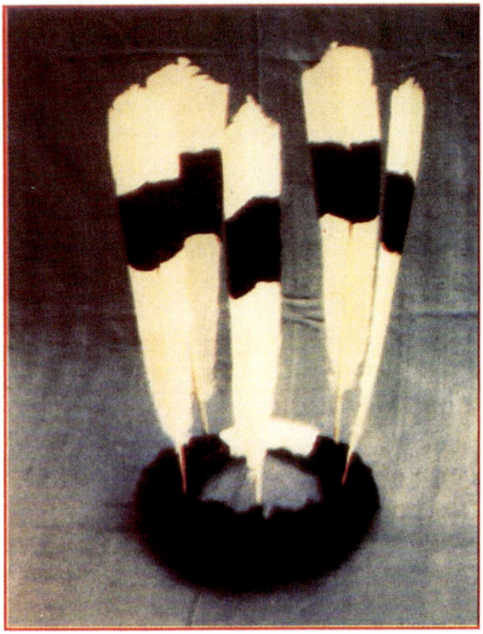

Fig. 1.2 : The Coronet

hair band as among the Maoris of New Zealand who use a hornbill feather to signify a person as a warrior. (The Ao Nagas by J.P. Mills, p. 45).

There is another type of coronet used by the tribals of Mon and Tuensang district of Nagaland. This type of coronet is also made of cane and orchid (red and yellow colour) in a conical shape slightly sloping from the top. The top of the coronet up to middle part is stitched with trimmed goat's hair. Two long tusks of wild boar are put in front side of the coronet. On important social functions and festivals, the Nagas put the most decorative coronet with hornbill feathers. This type of coronet is used by the tribes of Northern Nagaland such as the Phoms, the Konyaks, the Sangtams, the Yimchungers, the Changs and the Khiamungans particularly while dancing during the festivals. The Phoms, call their head-dress particularly when they fire their own made muzzle loaded guns at the time of festival dances. In fact, it is very popular among the Konyaks who fire guns at the time of dancing in unison with great joy. Such guns are manufactured locally.

There is yet another type of head-dress called '*Tsula*' used by the Angamis living in the Southern part of the State of Nagaland. This is made of bamboo slit, cotton and wool of different colours. This is exclusively used by the male member of the Angami tribe. By wearing '*Tsula*' at the time of dancing; the Angamis are looked like a group of peacock. It brings great charm to the spectators. The Zeliangs also have their distinctive head-dress made of bamboo, cotton and wool. They also put hornbill feathers on their coronet to make more attractive and beautiful as other tribals.

From the above presentation it is noted that the Nagas use different types of coronet as their head-dress which are made of different colourful objects demonstrating their culture. Such head-dresses are different in shapes, designs, colour and make from that of the other parts of the world which signifies the distinctiveness of Naga culture in terms of their crown. However, this beautiful part of Naga culture is disappearing slowly which needs to be revived in the context of present needs.

1.3 The Drongo Tail

Oyimki or Drongo's (a kind of leading small bird) tail is highly prized by the Nagas as an ornament. With the help of a thread which may be black, red, white or yellow in colour and one can make an ornament of this tail and be worn in the ear. The drongo is regarded as a special and peculiar bird because of its tail being sharp pointed uniformly.

That is why it is often equated with the value of a mithun or the head of a warrior.

This bird is the commander of a group of birds. It has sharp eyes and can be found all over the forest. To catch this bird, a special trap made of a women's hair is used, and it is during the time of flowering seasons of cotton and Elang trees which is the best time to catch this bird. It is such a difficult task to catch this bird. The tail part can make beautiful ornament. Therefore, the value of the tail of this bird becomes very costly as well as valuable.

Of course, bird's feathers have always been a part of the Naga traditional customs and culture, as in case of other tribes in other countries of the world. Some people use the feathers for their headgear. The women folk too use to insert it in their hair buns. The Nagas use such materials as ornaments putting in their coronet and also in their ears. Elsewhere, the feathers of the peacock, the bulbul, the partridge or other birds including the wildcock are also used for similar ornamental purposes. The Zeliangs use the feather of '*Nzie*' (Kelengleng, in Ao Naga, *Pezie* in Angami); the Rengmas use the feathers of *Azuzo* (bulbul) and *Atighi* (partridge).

In addition to the birds feathers, the Nagas also use small bundles of white cotton or even bark of the tree as ornaments in the ears.

The use of animal horns, especially the small round type of the mountain goat, is common as also the use of conch shells; cut into round shapes. This conch shell ornament is called Nangri by the Aos, Hangkap by Phoms and Dokchi by Changs. The natural objects that adorn the ears of Nagas are flowers and leaves on the one hand and the human hairs. The cotton flowers are worn by all the Nagas, called *Kumba Naro* in Ao, in fact those who cannot wear *Oyimki* have privilege to wear other items too. The cotton balls are commonly used by the Aos, the Semas and the Sangtams. The Nagas are fond of wearing the metallic ear ornaments. They also wear the trumpet shaped earring with small chains (six pices) hanging from circular part. It is generally made of copper. Then, there are brass earrings which are worn by the Lotha brides.

By and large, the Nagas use a variety of softwear for decorating their heads especially on the occasion of festivals.

1.4 The Boar Tusk Necklace

There are many kinds of animals on this earth both herbivorous and carnivorous, which provide men with meat and other valuable articles which are of great importance. Animal fur, skin, bones and teeth are being used as a part of thier dress from times immemorial and these animals paraphernalia complements the other decorative apparels made of gold, bronze and other precious metals.

The Naga traditional dress ensembles one variety and beauty. The tusk *shibu* of the boar makes it all more so, adding to its ever resplendent splendour. The Boar is an uncastrated pig and lives in the wild. It can be classified into two types: the first lives within a group which is called '*Pongisalu*' while the second lives isolated and alone. A group of boars can be easily tracked by its deep, characteristic grunt that rumbles through the forest at intermittent intervals and leads the hunter to it. The tusks obtained from these boars are used to decorate the headgear mostly by people in the Tuensang and Mon districts. Besides, Konyaks of Mon district, Chang, Phom, Yimchgunger of Tuensang district use boar tusks as necklace, but it is rarely worn, while the Aos and Semas use these as necklac. The lone boar is a dangerous animal and can be characterised by its nightly brawls. It also makes forays to the river source where it drinks and licks the mud in the twilight hours of the morning and midnight in '*Aiet*' where mud and salty water of red colour are found. These places are often used by the animals as their watering place. Here, the animals are killed easily by the hunter who lays trap and wait in a strategic position. Other methods are also employed to kill such dangerous animal and this include traps, guns or deep pits covered with foliage. The boar habitats beside slushy puddles resulting from alluvial deposits on the bank of rivers and it build its lair with grasses and dry vegetation closely resembling a nest. A hunting party may keep a close vigil on these boars at close distance and throw their spears together as the boar leaves its lair and thus kill it.

An elaborate scheme to capture the boar is devised by identifying jungle tracks used by them and digging about 10 feet deep pits under it. Pointed missiles, spikes, sticks are erected inside these pits and the pits are cleverly covered with thick foliage to give them a natural look. This process may take a short while and during the entire period co-habitation is restricted. Once the pits are completed and ready, it is visited at regular intervals to check the boars which might be trapped. An unsuspecting boar or a group of boars (if the hunter is lucky) may be easily deceived and may walk right into the trap or pit. A wounded boar is then an easy prey for the anxious hunters. The meat is equally distributed among the hunters and the tusk is awarded to the leader of the hunter. This is the traditional practice that has been followed all through the Naga history. The use of bows and traps are not very common among the Aos. Use of bows and arrows are more popular among the people of Mon and Tuensang, while Semas prefer local made traps.

Process of Making

The boar tusk is used as decorative ornament that is worn tightly around the neck (*Shibu* in Ao Naga). In the process of making such necklace, the materials such as thread, wood, cane, red cane, conch shell and round red beads are used. First of all, a piece of wood is tightly inserted into the hollow of the tusk leaving a part of the wood outside it. A knot made with plaited red cane is put where the piece of wood and the hollow portion of tusk are joined.

Some small holes are also made in the tusks through which cane fibre can tightly joined the two pairs of the tusks for the right side. In the same process the left side of the tusks are joined. In a boar tusk necklace, four tusks are used; two tusks for the right side and the other two for the left side. Again where four tusks are joined together, a flat piece of wood measuring two inches with two holes are put and over it a round shaped cut out of a conch shell is attached with small holes on it. Now again, two round red beads are required to put on the cut conch. This is called Gooseberry seeds (Lirjang). These two red beads and the cut out conch shell are tightened by cotton thread in the thin wool through the holes.

On the right side of the joined tusks, one end of the string it tied and the other end is tied in a round red bead with a round conch shell. On the left side of the joined tusks, a string is put like a hook and the two ends are crossed together with the help of conch shell on the right. To prevent movement here and there, a lever is put in the middle from right to left side of the necklace. It is now finished to be adorned on the neck. When it is worn on the neck, the string of the right and left sides crisscross so as not to let it fall down. But before using this tusk necklace it should be sanctified by a witch doctor *'arasentsur'*.

The advice of the local doctor, a witchcraft tells of good tidings with regard to children, longevity of life, expectancy etc. If the witchcraft sees some bad omens this kind of necklace is not purchased from others for use. The boar tusk is of two kinds: two joined tusk necklace is called *Ajapa* and the other four joined tusk necklace is called *Shipureb*. The first group is most ordinary whereas the second group is mostly worn by warriors who have excelled in the art of fighting. This tusk necklace can be worn by the Aos and the Semas. Only the warriors are entitled to use this type of necklace at the time of dancing. This tusk necklace is not only meant for festivals purpose but it can be used at normal times also. It can be sold and purchased without any restriction but before it is worn, at least a witchcraft doctor should be consulted whether the necklace is good or otherwise. Now-a-days, it is used for commercial purpose too.

1.5 The Conch Shell Necklace

Nagas are fond of sea shells, conch shells and snail shells etc. which are found on the sea-shore. Conch shell belongs to the Jimla family and closely resembles the '*Ongkok*' in colour and appearance. This is predominantly found in water of the South-West Asia like Arabian Sea, Gujarat Coast and the Gulf of Cambay etc. The conch shell which is called '*Lakumpong*' in Ao dialect, is made with the saliva, a kind of big snail which lives inside the conch shell. It always carries its shell even while searching for food in water.

The conch is characterised by its density and hardness. This is relatively rare as it is not found in all waters. The conch has different uses and this adds to its immense value. This is used as blow-horn in festive or worship times by many people. It is also used as a decorative piece at homes or can also be strung round as a necklace. People from the eastern parts of the world have exhibited a special fondness for this sea-shell only from distance places because of the absence of sea, ocean and great rivers in their country. They wore conch necklace from times immemorial, purchased from various places and many of them brought it from Burma.

This conch shell necklace is mainly for men. The Aos wear this necklace with great value. This necklace is completely a lace of sea-shore shells of different sizes. The centre of inner portion is known as '*Lakummulong*' and it is called '*Lakummulongzuk*'. While cutting this shell, lengthwise outer portion of the shell is cut off. This can be again cut into different shapes like round, rectangular etc. These items are worn by Naga women irrespective of status, high and low, rich or poor from times immemorial. This necklace is worn on the shoulder by some tribes, and other tribes adorn it on the chest mixed with other varieties of beads. Its length should be at least two inches to five inches long straight with small holes throughout its length.

This is the most valuable shell necklace worn by all Naga tribes and so it is common to all. The price of this necklace is very high because the conch shell is very difficult to get. The traders from Calcutta, Madras and Bombay use to bring this shell towards north-east India where it is used with great value. It is also brought from across the country like Burma, Thailand etc.

Naga society had experienced many upheavals since the advent of Christianity. Perhaps, the saddest part is the gradual and steady erosion of traditional values. The Christian missionaries did not encourage to preserve the rich Naga culture. As a result, almost all the cultural artifacts especially the most valuable ornamental items started disappearing from Naga society. Now-a-days, the original conch necklace is very difficult to get and it is very expensive too. It is mostly worn by the women folk of Angami, Chakhesang and Rengma tribes. The Angami women wear this necklace alongwith other necklace and this presents a very pretty look. All cultural ensemble would be incomplete without the glimmering conch necklace, which enhances a maiden's beauty. A maiden decked in this finery and presenting her soul catching repertoire of folk songs present a very ethereal picture and this sight is so beautiful that it is almost divine. The use of this necklace is also very much prevalent among the Chakhesang women especially in tribal dances. The Sema women do wear it during the '*Tuluni*' festival and this suits them very beautifully. This is also worn by the women of Zeliang tribe. The conch necklace is rated as the best among all the traditional finery. In Tuensang district, all the five tribes use different dresses like other people of Nagaland. However, they don't wear conch shell necklace as worn by the other tribes. They use bear's nails and tiger's teeth necklaces instead of conch shell. The Changs call them '*Eiksen*' and '*Saonyu*' respectively.

Each of such traditional dress possesses a decorative body gear indicating a sign of great value and prestige. Among the Aos, the '*Lankummulong*' exactly hold this exalted position. Consequently, there is a strict etiquette which has to be adhered too. Only the rich and that too only the male member of the family and their offerings are allowed to wear it. This precludes all the women folk, and other male members who might have excelled themselves in the art of warfare. The conch is strung through a thread and it is worn by draping it across one shoulder and guiding it right below the other arm running almost as low as the sides of the abdomen. This represents a unit or one laces of conches. The common practice among the rich is to wear one or two strings of conches across both the shoulder. A son or a grandson of a rich parent is entitled to wear these laces by virtue of his parents/grandparents affluence. A rich man is allowed to a maximum of three braid of conches but the normal practice is to wear two of them. A young lad wearing two of these ornamental pieces is a sure sign that both his father and grandfather were rich people. A single braid of conches looks effeminate on the person wearing it so people strive towards achieving the status that would permit them to wear two. This gives an idea of the great significance attached to the act of wearing two conch laces.

Naga culture is very rich in itself. The use of decorated coronet, the boar tusk necklace, the conch shell etc. are some of the examples unlike many other people of different countries. Unfortunately, many of such valuable items are slowly disappearing due to impact of Christianity and modernisation. Many youngsters are not aware of the essence of cultural value and its significance in their society. It is a great challenge for the Nagas to preserve and maintain their cultural heritage.

1.6 The Cornelian Shell Necklace

God created man in his own image and left this world to be inhabited by beautiful people. Man's ingenuity is clearly manifested in the dresses he creates to cover his body and his sense of esthetics is reflected in the ornaments he adorns. Of course, the differences in the physical attributes of man and woman also necessitates differences in attire, and on festive occasions one has to create a special look. The feathers, necklaces, specially woven fabric are on display and both men and women decorate themselve. the Cornelian shell necklace '*Marzuk*' is a special kind of necklace with its abundance of colour and artistic harmony, is undoubtedly one of the most beautiful necklace worn by the Nagas. It is commonly used by the Aos.

Process of Making

This necklace requires special type of conch shell, beads cornelian stones and bones. In the process of making the following steps are followed:

(i) In the first place, eight to ten conch shells are required for making two parallel strings which will be hung over the neck on the back shoulder. Actually, only the core portion of the shell is utilised and the rest is discarded. The preparation of the conch shell is not easy. It requires a fair amount of skill.

Also, fairly strong strings are required so that it can withstand the weight of many heavy beads.

(ii) Having prepared these conch strings, two pieces of flat rectangular animal bones about two inches long and half an inch thick are required. Small holes are drilled on the bones through which the strings of conch shell and the lower beads can be tied.

(iii) While the upper portion of the necklace has conch shell the lower portion constitutes four or five strings of red cornelian cut stones, and the lower portion is connected with the upper portion through a middle portion which is a set of black and white porcelain clay beads are used. About fifty precious cornelian stones are required for one necklace (8 to 10 each string). With these, '*Marzuk*' becomes the most valuable ornament. It is specially reserved for festivities. It is said that these cornelian stones are found in ocean beds. Their extraction is an arduous task. In India, Gujarat is famous for it. The stones are cut in hexagonal fashion and are like small prisms with holes in the centre through which the string can be passed.

(iv) As mentioned above, there is a bone which connects the upper portion with the middle and lower portion. To add to the beauty of this bone, a small marble like bead is attached in the middle on the top side.

When a '*Marzuk*' is made and hung over the neck, it reaches upto the navel, and the five strings cover a fair portion of the body above it. This is mostly worn by the Aos, but in the other tribes of Central and Southern Nagaland (Angamis, Rengmas, Lothas, Semas) there is no restriction and even women folk can wear it. It is generally inherited only by the eldest male member of the family and if there is none, the nearest male relative may inherit the same.

In the past, the Nagas penetrated the trade links with the South-East Asia via Burma and many of these shells and stones were brought from that side. After consolidation of ties with India, the trade has also shifted and now these objects are being obtained from cities like Calcutta, Madras, Bombay, Banaras. In the past, the Angami traders of Khonoma were more active and ventured trips upto Longkhum and beyond for trading such precious objects.

After the advent of British, several changes had taken place. However, the British were not against the traditional practices of the Nagas. The *Gaon Boras* and the *Dobashis* were allowed to wear their necklaces. It is for this reason that *'Marzuk'* was also called the '*Dobashi*' necklace. Use of such necklace is a part of material culture. There is a need to preserve such items of cultural artifact too.

1.7 The Head Plate

A person, while choosing or designing a dress for his personal use, normally assumes that it will gather appreciation from others as the proverb says 'eat according to your own choice but wear according to the choice of others in society'. Perhaps, this is the reason why a person wear a given dress with societal approval. It is again true that every individual puts some speciality based on his own liking in order to be conspicuous, impressive and outstanding in a group or a gathering. Similarly every society while approving or disapproving any dress, fashion or an attire look into a very important factor i.e. to what extent the same reflects the societal values, culture and heritage. May be for such reason, such dress for example *sari, longi* or gown is worn in different styles in different societies. It signifies certain societal status or position in a given society.

Similarly, the 'head plate' is one of the most important dresses of the Nagas having a lot of significance to one's personal traits and achievement and also to the societal values. An attempt is made here to describe its design, process of making, value and beliefs; associated with it. Special reference is given here to the head plate of the Ao Nagas.

Design and Process of Making

Though the head plate is a single object, it can be described as having five distinctive parts from design and stages of making point of view and the cover to protect it from any possibility of damage. All these five parts are described below:

1. *The main head plate:* It is the most important part of the head plate, designed to symbolise a human head. It is designed in a tidious process with the help of the following materials:

(a) A flat (of around 1 cm in thickness) uniformly double concave plane wooden plate of around 14 to 15 inches in length 4 inches in width at both the ends and $2^{1/2}$ inches at the mid point.
(b) A thin (of round 4 mm thickness) uniformly double concave

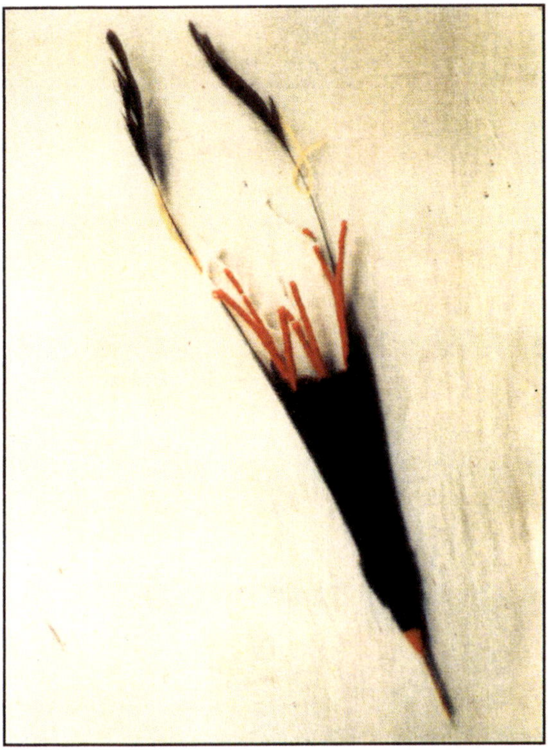

Fig. 1.3 : The Drongo Tail

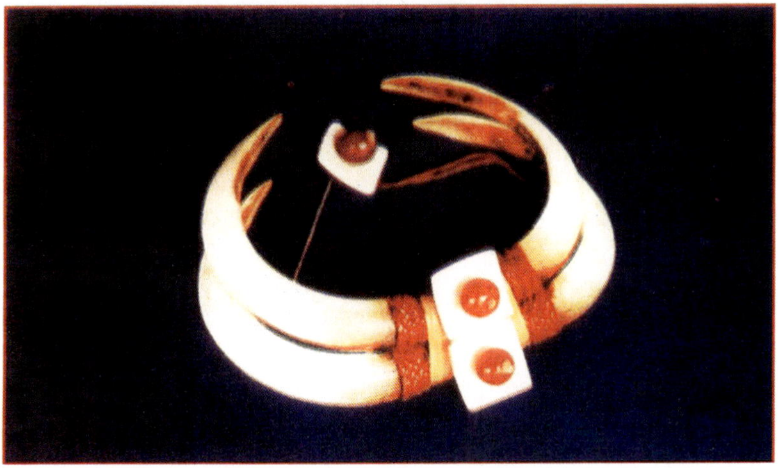

Fig. 1.4 : The Boar Tusk Necklace

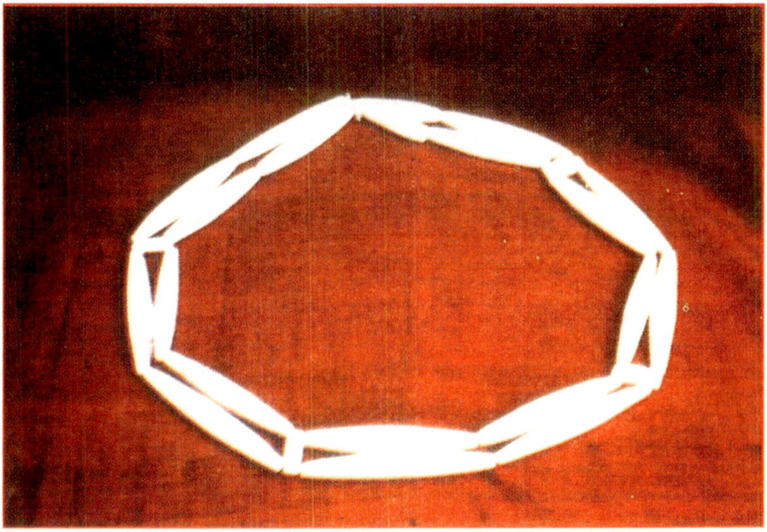

Fig. 1.5 : The Conch Shell Necklace

Fig. 1.6 : The Cornelian Shell Necklace

place bamboo plate exactly of the same length with the wooden plate but of different width i.e. round $1^{1/2}$ inches at both the ends and only 1/2 inch at the middle.

(c) Thin and long red coloured cane splints of around 2 mm width (through indigenous colouring process).

(d) Thin yellow orchid splints of two different width: one set of 2 mm width and the other set of 1 cm width.

(e) Cowries of uniform length around 1/2 inch (approximately 100 in numbers)

(f) White threads.

Initially, the flat wooden plate is polished by means of sandy leaves; a jungle leaf called *"Poktsukue (rarawa)"* in Ao, that works as the sandy paper. Then small holes of around 1 mm radius are made at a regular interval of around 1/2 inch in a curve 1/2 inch below the upper edge of the wooden plate. Similar holes at similar intervals are made in a curve below the first line of holes in such a way that the middle space is uniformly double concave to exactly accommodate the double concave flat wooden plate 1/2 inch (exactly the length of the cowries) below the second line of holes another parallel line of holes are made at similar intervals in such a way that the joining two corresponding holes makes a right angle with the tangent drawn at the mid point of the curve to tie the cowries in a way that two corresponding belly lines of cowries will be parallel. The cowries of equal length are choosen and the belly sides are horizontally cut in order to keep them flat exposing their mouth line, up to the face of the wooden plate. Both the sides of the cowries are rubbed in a flat sand stone, so that when two cowries are placed side by side; there remains no gap in between. Around fifty cowries (as many as the holes) are placed one by one in two rows (above the first line of holes and between two parallel lines of holes). Both the rows of cowries are convex towards the flat bamboo plate to be placed in between. The setting of cowries takes place with the help of a needle and strong white thread. First the thread on the backside of the wooden plate is taken through the extreme hole of the upper line of hole, then the thread through the hole of the cowries, passes over its lower end to go back to the backside of the plate to tie the upper end of the cowries in a similar way. The upper end of the cowries are kept at the same level with the edge of the plate. The thread is again brought down upto the hole with a single round over the up going thread moving horizontally upto the next hole in order to tie the next cowries on the similar way. The second row of cowries are also set in the similar process between two parallel line of holes. The process of setting up cowries is undertaken with skills and care so that no thread is exposed over the face of the cowries, and all thread movements are visible on the backside of the plate. The two row of cowries symbolise the exposed teeth of the human head.

Now-a-days, cowries are brought from Calcutta, Madras, and Bombay and sold in Nagaland markets. But one wonders how the hill people used cowries in the past in Nagaland where cowries were not available. Infact the Nagas were using cowries and some other sea products in their traditional attires. It is told that in olden days when some Nagas had gone to the coastal part of South Asia (Bay of Bengal) they found cowries in the sea shore. They bought cowries and started using in their dresses. These cowries are called *Molo-ipa* which means "sea teeth" (*Molo* means sea and *ipa* means teeth). In the early part of the century, the cowries were supplied by the traders who had migrated from "Mann" (presently Myanmar). In the middle part and later part of the century, cowries were procured by the Angamib traders particularly from Khonoma village and supplied to the other parts of Naga country for making attires.

In the next step, the tongue, made of bamboo plate, orchid and cane splints are kept in between the two jaws of teeth. The bamboo plate is set and tied tightly by means of thread at five places using the holes of the wooden plate, at both the ends and three other places with equal distance. Yellow orchid and red cane splints are woven over the bamboo plate to add colour to the tongue. These splints are prepared in a tidious process. The yellow rochid is cut and dried up for at least fifteen days under bright sunshine. The more it is dried, the more yellow it becomes. Then it is kept in water for a day or two and after that it is opened with a sharp knife in order to clear the inner soft portion and leave the skin undamaged. Then it is split longitudinally for making splints of around 2 mm length. The cane splints are also prepared by means of a sharp *dao* or knife. A long matured cane is longitudinally split into several pieces in order to get the splints of around the same width with orchid splints. The inner part is then cleared by a sharp *dao* or knife using the thumb and adjacent finger. The splints are held in the left hand and the knife in the right. The cutting edge of the knife is kept pressed against the inner side of the cane while the fore finger is kept just beneath the splint below the knife. Then the splint is drawn outward with the help of the left hand while the knife is pressed on the splint and pushed inward with the right thumb. It is repeated several times but only on the inner side, because the outer skin for drying must remain undamaged. The red cane splints are then used horizontally and the yellow orchid vertically in the process of weaving a wavy check pattern. Over both the ends of weaving over the bamboo plate; two thin yellow orchid strips of around 1 cm width is wrapped with some paste or adhesive so that the strips adhere to the bamboo plate protecting the terminals of the weaving works. The bamboo plate with the colourful weaving work symbolises the tongue. This tongue is kept in between the row of cowries because when the hunter brings the chopped head; it is always found that half of the tongue comes outside after being clamped between two jaws of teeth.

In the next step, three bunches of long (7 to 8) goat's hair (coloured with red in the same process as cane splints, (to be discussed later) are put on the horizontal ends of the wooden plate; two bunches under the two extreme cowries of both the jaws, and the other bunch under the tongue. The long hairs keep swing on both the sides to symbolise blood strained ears of the chopped head.

2. *The Blood Lines*: Blood line is nothing but a series of bunches of long goat's hair held by a thin bamboo chord with the help of circular cane hooks set in the bunch. From blood line point of view, the head plate is classified into two categories; i.e. the layered head plate and double line head plate. In case of single layered head plate, only one line of long goat's hair (around 7 to 8 inches) is set above the first line in such a way that the loose end of the bunches of the second later overlaps the roots of the first line of longer goat's hair bunches.

The blood line is considered to have two main functions; firstly, to symbolise the stream of blood coming, secondly, to make the war dance colourful with the rythmical swings of the blood lines. The goat's hair is deliberately kept long to swing in the air to demonstrate how the blood strings out of the human head when it is cut suddenly by means of a sharp *dao.* In a special occasion, when 30 to 40 persons wearing the head plate gather in a semicircular line to perform war dance, the rythmical swing of the blood lines in a series look like a rainbow and brings charm to the spectators.

Though the blood line has been described as a single series of goat's hair bunched, the design and making process involves tedious work. The making process involves goat hair dyeing, bunching by putting a circular hook inside, orchid wrapping and setting up the bunches on a bamboo stick etc. Partially, the thin cane strings are prepared with the help of a sharp *dao* or knife and then the circular hook strings (just look like screen hooks used at the terminals of window screen chord) are made out of it by screwing over a round bamboo stick clockwise leading 6 or 7 times. These hooks are put at the root of the bunches in such a way that only circular rings are exposed outside (uniformly so that one stick can go inside all the hooks in a series to hold all the bunches) and the rest part is hidden inside the bunch. This multiple wrapping covers around 1 cm on the root of the bunch. Wrapping of black or red thread if exposed; looks ugly and therefore, is covered with shining yellow orchid strips of around 1 cm in width. The process of wrapping requires special technique. First, both the ends of the strips (of side 1½ cm × 1 cm) are folded into the length of the folded strip and it is just equal to the perimeter of the cylindrical root of the bunch of goat hair. A black or red thread in 'U' shape is then inserted in such a way that both the side threads touch the folding lines of the strip. Then, the end of the bunch of goat hair with the circular hook is kept over it and the upper part of the 'U' shaped thread is just inserted around the hook. After that, both the loose ends of the thread are pulled down making a knot. When the knot is put, the root of the bunch, wrapped with black or red cotton thread is automatically covered by the yellow orchid strip exposing only the circular hook. The surplus thread is then cut off and the bunch becomes ready to be set on the bamboo stick. This bamboo stick is slightly curved in a convex manner. The perimeter of the base of this cylindrical bamboo stick is slightly smaller than the perimeter of the hook bacause it has to go inside the circular hook. One by one, the bunches are set by means of a bamboo stick and a red thread in such a way that no space is allowed in between two adjacent bunches. In a standard head plate, the number of such bunches accommodated on the bamboo stick is around eighty to eighty-five. Another long red thread is used for tying the bunches at the end point of their respective orchid strip. In order to fix the blood line on the head plate, 8 small holes at equal interval from one end to the other are made just above the lower edge line of the wooden plate. The blood line is then fixed on the wooden plate by tying tightly with the 8 holes. Since, the independent knots are put at each hole, the extended thread of the knots are cut off. This is how the single blood line is fixed on the head plate. In order to bring uniformity in length, the goat hair ends are horizontally sized in a line by means of a sharp *dao.*

In the case of a single layered bloodline, since the circular hooks touch the lower side surface of the wooden plate, a portion on the face of the wooden plate remains naked without any decorative work. Sometimes, to cover this naked part of the head plate another layer of blood line is set above the lower bloodline, as discussed above and in this case the head plate is classified as double layered head plate.

The second bloodline is prepared in similar process and with similar techniques differs from the first layer in the length of the goat hair used. The sized goat hair bunch in case of second layer measures around an inch in length just to cover the naked part of the main head plate up to the beginning of the orchid wrapping off the lower bloodline. The second bloodline is then placed on the naked part of the head plate by making few holes above the line of holes meant for the lower bloodline. A red thread is used to tie it tightly with the holes made for it and the lower line of holes used for the lower line of cowries. The stick holding the circular hooks of the second bloodline is bent downwardly concave curve in order to touch the lower end of all the cowries of the lower jaw.

The most important and interesting phenomenon is the indigenous process of colouring the goat hair to be used for the purpose of head plate. The person, who performs the colouring process maintains purity for atleast six days before he commences the process. It is dangerous to deviate from the rule of purity because, it is believed that when a person violates this rule, he will either have short life or misfortune will occur in the family or the colour may fade away after a few months.

The materials used for colouring process are (1) rice beer, (2) *Wati* root (a creeper), (3) *Tangshi* (a sour fruit leave of fruit skin), (4) *Tangmo* fruit skin and (5) pure water from jungle. The process of colouring is not performed at home or in the village for they believe that if someone knows it or witness it, the colour will not be deep red. For this reason, they perform the process of colouring secretly in the deep forest particularly at a place which is unaccessible to others. Without informing anyone at home; (except his wife) he moves to the forest along with the ingredients and other needful articles such as *dao,* an earthen pot and flenching stone (for making new fire in the traditional way). First, he cuts some tree branches and fence to protect the process of making from the eyes of others. Then, making a new fire place to make new fire is made for the purpose. After making the new fire, he puts the earthen pot with water, rice beer and all other ingredients as stated above. When the water with all the ingredients starts boiling; goat hair and cane splints are put into the earthen pot and boiled for one or two hours; and automatically the colour of the goat hair and cane splints are changed into deep red. When the water cools down, these materials are taken out for washing and kept hanging for drying.

Now, the colour is permanent and does not fade away even after forty/ fifty years. The colour that is available in present market can hardly match the colour brought in the indigenous method of dyeing and colouring. The colour so obtained may be varied because of the variation in the proportion of the ingredients and the quality of making.

3. *The Pluralisors*: On both the ends of the upper surface of the main head plate; two small rows of goat hair bunches are put which are termed as *Pluralisors.* (in Ao it is called *Mangko talila* which means additional heads). The *Pluralisors* indicate that the user has hunted several human heads (at least two) to his credit. In the absence of two *Pluralisors* it is regarded that the user of the head plate has got only one head to his credit. The *Pluralisors* on the main head plate look like rabbit ears. These are made in the similar process as in the case of bloodlines. The difference is that, the bamboo stick holes only 10 to 11 bunches of goat hair (the length of *Pluralisor* being around 1 1/2 inches can accommodate only that number of bunches). The length of the goat hair is exactly same as in case of the second layer of bloodline. The *Pluralisors* are set with the support of two thin cane sticks fixed on the respective ends of the upper surface like a goal post in football ground. The cane stick (around 3 inches long) is bent with right angles at two points 1/2 inch from the ends. The two side ends are fixed on the respective ends of the upper surface of the main head plate. The cane sticks are fixed in such a way that when the bunches of goat hair are upward set, the horizontal sides remain at height equal with the upper end of the orchid wrapping. A strong white thread is used to tie all the bunches with the cane stick and the line of holes meant for the upper line of cowries.

4. *The Tying String*: It is used in the head plate as supporting component. The main function of tying string is to tie the head plate on the neck of the user in order to keep the head plate on the shoulder. It is made of black cotton, woollen thread; and the making process is very simple. The thread is doubled and redoubled in order to make it thick and soft. This tying string is taken through another strong cotton ring made with black cotton thread through a small hole on the mid point of the wooden plate; just below the upper line of cowries and above upper edge of the tongue. The small ring is used in order to hang the head plate on the tying string to be fastened on the neck. Both the ends of the tying string hangs on the chest like tie. They tied string, because of its softness, and knot on the back side of the neck does not create any problem to the user even if he wears it for longer period of time.

5. *The Cover*: It is again an additional part of the head plate prepared and used to protect the head plate from dust, smoke and other dirts. This cover is made out of long cane sticks and young bamboo bark. The cane sticks are arranged systematically to make a rectangle. Once a rectangular net like structure is made, barks are placed over it and stitched. In the similar way another leaf plate is made. The leaf plate is made as big as to cover the whole head plate. Then both the lief plates are kept on both the sides of the plates and at regular interval the leaf plates are tied up, with threads in order to act as guard plates on either sides of the head plate. The head plate, since considered as one of the most costliest costumes of a male Naga, is kept with maximum care. Unlike their shield, it is not hanged on the wall of the kitchen. It is kept in a small room which is usually constructed at one of the corner of the kitchen opposite the fireplace. The head plate is kept in a small room to protect from dust and smoke coming out of the kitchen.

Significance: Head hunting was almost a common practice in olden days among the Nagas society. This was a part of their socio-cultural practice in those days. To cut a human head in a raid was the greatest honour for a warrior. In this way he earns the title to wear particular dresses and ornaments. The commoners, those who failed to hunt human head were considered inferior and the right to wear the warrior dresses were not allowed to them.

Head plate is an important component of a warrior dress. It conveys the message that the wearer has the credit of taking atleast one human head in a raid. The presence of *Pluralisors* on both the ends of the main head plate symbolises that the users has hunted more than one head. It is an additional achievement for the warriors to his credit.

The Head plate looks very beautiful and it makes the very commanding with honour gathering of hundred, a few persons are found wearing such head plate. These people catch the eyes of others and at every stage of social function, they are highly respected. Many people may wish to wear such plate to demand special respect; but he cannot do so, unless he had hunted at least one head. Head hunting was not an easy task. It requires war skills, strength, strategic move and with determination right from childhood, the Naga boys start learning war tactics to become a warrior and head hunter so, that they can earn the title to use special dresses like head plate and hornbill feathers and so on. That is why, the use of head plate had become a rated social status among the Nagas.

The head plate has another significance too. In a group of head hunters dance the rhythmic swing of deep red coloured goat hair along with their rhythmic dance looks majestic and the spectators enjoys with artistic values.

Like batches, stars, strips and cross swords are used in army uniform to signify the rank, experience and achievement of an army officer, the head plate was used by the Naga warrior as a symbol to state his achievements in the past raids. The head plate thus, was considered as one of the most honourable achievements and motivator for young warriors.

The Extent of Use: The head plate is used by the male warrior of the Naga society exclusively by those who have the credit of hunting at least one human head in a raid. Other persons or ordinary male members of the society were not entitled to wear the head plate. For a weak and coward person (unskilled with war techniques) the use of head plate was like a dream. At the same time, all Naga tribes do not use this head plate as component of their tribal costume. The tribes who were using this head plate as part of their traditional dress are, the Angamis, the Aos, the Semas and the Lothas. The process of making, the design and the style of weaving are different from one to another tribe.

The Head plate of the Angamis is more attractive and beautiful. It is a circular type with colourful materials. They put it horizontally on their chest, they call it '*Thacu*'. The Semas also wear head plate that is similar to the head plate as mentioned above. The Semas are fond of this head plate much. In the past the Aos, who did not know how to make it, purchased from others by giving them a few basket of paddy. They call it '*Kupdang*' in Ao dialect.

The head plate was not used daily. It was mostly used in some important festivals. In Ao community, it was worn specially at the time of dancing in the festivals particularly '*Moatsu*' and '*Tsungremong*' and on the day of *mithun* sacrifice in the village. Similarly, the Sema users were using their head plates on their important festivals. Now, the noted village where it is found in good number is '*Longkhum*' because there were many head-hunters in those days and many of them could make this plate. They were wearing this attire during festivals and local ceremonies. Now-a-days, any person who got it or who can buy or make it can use without restriction because the system of its entitlement, as found in the traditional society has already been changed. However, the right of entitlement to use the head plate was strictly followed during head hunting days. When the practice of head hunting was banned by the British colonial rule, the binding of entitlement was also relaxed. Many Nagas went to European countries during the First

World War as labourers and many of them participated in Kuki and Apur Expeditions and were allowed to use this head plate. Subsequently, ordinary people who could manage, to get it started using this attire at the time of festival dances.

During the days of head hunting practices, the use of head plate with or without *pluralisors* was so terrifying to the opponent warrior. When a warrior with the head plate is defeated, the winner first cut his head and then if time permits, (before the group members of the defeated warriors came running to attack him) he takes out all his ornaments and dresses including the head plate. Other members of the winner's party cut the palm and feet to show their participation in the head hunting. When the head hunter takes out the head plate of the deceased warrior he did not use it immediately. After the war is over, one festival is arranged in the village, and in that festival, he shows the head plate to a fortune teller and request him to sanctify it. The fortune teller by examining the head plate will give comments as to whether it will be good to use it or not. In case he is satisfied that there is no bad sign with the head plate, he sanctifies it to be used without fear. In this way, many warriors were found having more than four to five head plate in Naga society.

As stated above, the Naga head plate was considered as one of the most valuable items and male dresses in traditional Naga society. Because it signifies not only the status of a warrior, but it brings glory and honour to a man in society.

Unfortunately, the techniques of making such a valuable dress is forgotten by many people. The Naga indigenous dyeing method, designing and also the process of making has almost forgotten by many people.

Most of the Naga master craftsmen had already died. And unfortunately the youngsters have not yet learned the techniques of making such costly valuable dress. Many are also not aware about its scope and utility in the context of present society. Such dresses which were manufactured by means of simple *dao,* bare handed in the past can be manufactured with the help of modern machines today.

Once it is produced fixing lower rate at larger scale by modernising the process of making, a lot of revenues can be earned. It has high export potential especially in the international market once it is taken up in the right direction replacing the traditional methods of making by modern scientific methods. Such ornamental items once they are popularised in the international world markets; the identity of the Nagas will be known in different foreign countries. However, it depends on how the Nagas take care about their culture and use it for a desirable change in the right perspective.

1.8 The Cowries Apron

According to the Bible, God created man to be unclothed and to remain pure and undefiled. But, Adam and Eve, became conscious of their nakedness, when they disobeyed God. As a result, they hastened to cover themselves with leaves. This is considered to be the first fashion of human dress. With the passage of time, different dresses were created and the man and woman began to make themselves distinct. Among the Nagas too, from the earliest time, the man had their own loin cloth and the women had skirts. The loin cloth often takes the form of an apron. Here we shall look closely to an apron studded with several cowries which is commonly worn during the festivals.

This type of apron may differ from tribe to tribe. Among the Angamis, the Chakhesangs and the Zeliangs, this dress can be called as loin cloth. Because, it is wrapped around the hip leaving no part exposed; whereas among other tribes, including the Aos, it is worn covering only the front side of the body. The former loin cloth also reaches right upto the knees whereas in the apron type it is shorter. Such aprons are of different types with different designs. Some aprons are narrow and long one whereas some are shorter and broader with different colours. To ensure the apron stretch well, some tribes attach small brass piece and some tribes put cowries.

The cowries are small oval shaped sea shells with a slit opening on one side. These belong to the family of mollusk and are found along the coastal sea shores everywhere especially Arabian sea, Bay of Bengal, Indian Ocean etc. These cowries are collected from the sea and are buried under the earth for a definite period of time till such time, the animals inside the shells are killed. Later they are dug out again and cleaned for ornamental purpose.

The Process of Making

The first thing required is a piece of cloth. Before starting the process of making such dress, the maker should strictly follow the rules of obtaining from sex; maintaining as per the established custom. This piece is then cut in the form of a hexagon, and the top side is curved like an arch through which the cane belt can be put in. The vertical length will be around 30 inches (two and half feet), whereas as the middle portion will be around 13-14 inches. The bottom horizontal side is around 12 inches, whereas the top side is around 11 inches. This apron has three distinct portions as described below.

The Top Portion

On the top portion, three arches are made with red coloured thread. Below these arches, the cowries are studded in two curved rows that are parallel to the arches. In the centre, four cowries are studded like the petals of flower.

The Middle Portion

In the middle portion, the cowries are put in a vertical fashion (with slits upright). They are put closely to one another so that no empty place is left. On the side of this rectangular portion, are tufts of goat hair dyed into red bunches which are attached with the help of small yellow coloured orchid stems. The process of dyeing of orchid stem is illustrated under the item 'The Sash' in serial No. 11. The middle portion is entirely studded with about 500-600 cowries.

The Lower Portion

This is the largest portion and comprises of more than half of the apron. It is divided into four portions and about 500-600 cowries are put horizontally close to one another with a strong thread. Thus, a standard apron of such type will require 1000-1200 cowries. The materials are now ready and can be folded from the bottom and top sides with the middle intact. We, now, have a most beautiful cultural dress which is really popular among the Aos, the Semas, the Lothas and the Rengmas. The women folk are not allowed to touch such dress. Such aprons were worn only by those men who were excellent warriors. On festive occasions it adds a lot of attraction. It moves the spectators with joy since this dress was first made popular among the Aos of Longkhum village, it is often called Longkhum *Zubu* (*Langtem.*). The Semas call it *'Amini Kuda'*, Yimchunger, Khiamngan, Sangtam and Chang use decorated festival aprons with cowries and Job's tear seeds. This apron is rectangular in shape and its whole length is nearly a foot long 7 to 8 inches wide. But this apron is not similar with that type used by the Aos, Lothas, Rengmas and the Semas respectively. In the middle portion, they put a beautiful thin round bell which produces a tingling sound while dancing. This decorated apron is called *Lamei* and as *Laa* in Chang dialect. Unfortunately only few people can make such dress today, and it is gradually disappearing.

A tremendous change is undergoing in Naga society today due to the impact of modern education and Christianity. The outlook of a tribal Naga has already been changed totally. The head-hunting practice and *mithun* feast celebration is no more in their society.

The aspects of both material and non-material culture of the Nagas are gradually disappearing, which is highly regrettable. Unfortunately, no such systematic documentation work have so far been undertaken by any agency.

1.9 The Dao-Holder

In a traditional Naga family, every male member use to keep atleast one *dao* each with *dao*-holder. It is considered to be shameful if they don't maintain it properly. A *dao* holder can keep the *dao* intact and can carry it safely. It can be called either a *dao*-holder or a *dao*-case; the latter is used by the people of Tuensang district. The women folk may use the *dao* as a tool in their day-to-day work; but the *dao*-holder or the *dao*-case is only for men folk according to their custom. The *dao* box is made of special quality wood *Eku Atsuyimbang* and *Oze* wood (Ao names). This wood is also used for making utensils like spoon, cup, fork etc. and such quality woods are available throughout Nagaland.

The Process of Making

For making a *dao*-holder, only the best quality of wood is selected. A *dao* holder is around six to seven inches long and has a vertical slit in which the *dao* can be put with the blade downwards and the handle upwards. The *dao* holder or case which is used in Tuensang district is much larger and is more like a case or cover. A *dao* is then put there in the backside of the body in vertical position. Thus, there is a little difference between a *dao*-holder which is used in Mokokchung district and a *dao* case or cover use in Tuensang district. The process of making and its design is also different as stated below.

Type-1: Sketches of Various Stages

(i) The first step involves the selection of a piece of wood. A

Fig. 1.7 : The Head Plate

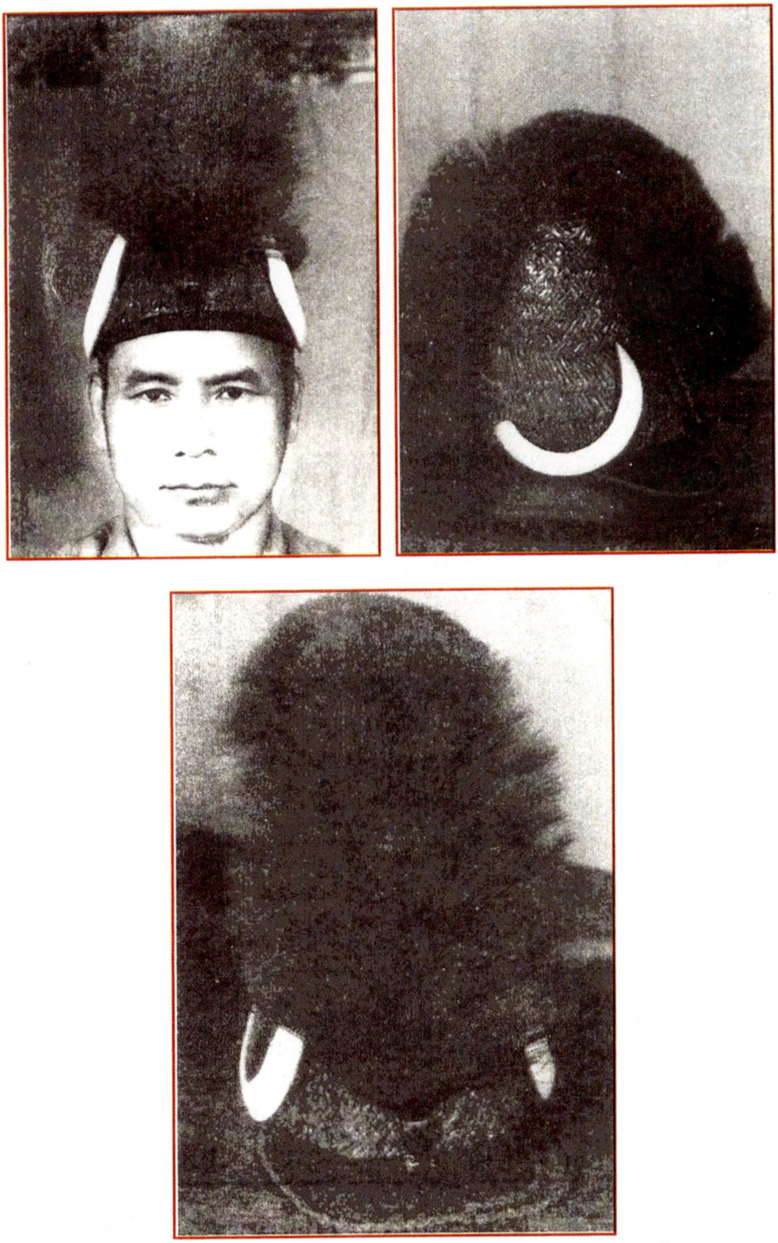

Fig. 1.8 : The Cowries Apron

Fig. 1.9A : The Dao-Holder

Fig. 1.9B : The Dao-Holder

solid piece cut in the form of a cuboid which is 7 × 2½ × 2 inches is adequate, although the size of the person and the *dao* are important considerations.

(ii) A vertical slit is to be made in the centre, and this slit is fairly long (about five inches) leaving an equal margin on both sides. The width is such that the blade can pass freely through the hole which is about half an inch. The slit is made from top to bottom with a sharp chisel with a wooden hammer.

(iii) Now, we have to make a parallel horizontal slit on the back side through which the belt can be passed so that the holder can be tied to the waist. This slit is made into two stages. In the first stage, we have to create a hollow rectangular space in the middle. This is about $3^{1/2}$ inches long and 1 inch wide and its depth is less than half an inch.

(iv) Two slits have to be made on each side which will be connected tc the hollow rectangular portion. As a result, we have a long slit running along the entire length of the holder, but only the middle portion is hollow with three sides removed whereas in the side slits the back portion is left intact to provide a hold for the belt. The hollow portion in the middle is helpful for adjusting the belt, but the sides provide the support. (see the sketch diagram).

(v) Now, we have to create the slanting side surface and the concave front with curved sides. First, the sides are given a gentle slanting shape with the result that the cuboid looks like a trapezium whose top is shorter than the base. Then the front portion is hollowed into a concave form with the help of the chisel. This is a delicate job and needs to be done very carefully so that the surface is concave with maximum depth towards the central portion. In addition, the horizontal and vertical sides of the originally rectangular face are also to be curved like gentle arches. This demands to be smoothened with the help of special kind of leaf known as *Poktsukve* in Ao dialect. The leaves are finer than the best sand paper and especially suitable for the job.

(vi) While the *dao*-holder is ready after the above stages are completed, for festive purposes it is important to have some engravings which add to its beauty and significance. For example, we create small circles sitting over reverse conical structures. These resemble the pictures of men with the circle as the head and the cone as the body.

In addition, we can have crisscross designs which resemble woven fabric. To add the beauty, indigenous red colour could be put on the object so that everyone feels attracted.

Type II

In this type, the main difference is that this has to be used vertically and is generally much bigger. Its length may be as much as ten inches and its width five to six inches. The other difference as pointed before is that the vertical slit stops short of the baseline by nearly an inch and the slit in effect becomes likewise in its width too, a margin of half an inch or more may be left on each side. The horizontal slit, although of the same type of structure as in Type I with a hollow middle portion, is smaller than in the former type. The main difference is in the aesthetic outer appearance in the middle portion of the front concave surface, a one inch bone is put horizontally. All along the sides a border is created in which small holes are drilled through which tuffs of black human hair and red dyed goat hair are tied to add to its beauty.

An important difference between the two types are that, while the user draws his *dao* out of the holder by taking his hand behind his waist and towards the back sideways, in the second type of holder the hand is flung from over the shoulder to reach the handle which is being supported by the spinal cord. Infact, this pattern of use requires the larger size of the *dao*-holder.

Finally, it is important to mention that the *dao*-holder or the *dao*-case need the belt which is woven by the women. This belt or string is called *Nokleptsuyu* in Ao language. These belts are beautifully decorated with cowries and jobs tears shells. Also, strong bones are used as clasps or hook and these are stitched on each end.

The *dao*-case worn on the back occupies the space just above the buttocks and positioned against the spinal cord which helps the men to maintain a straight posture as well.

As mentioned earlier, the *dao* is a part and parcel of Nagas life, for he may use it while farming, climbing hills, trees or clearing the jungle, or even as a tool for fighting. In head-hunting days it was used for chopping the head of the enemy. Infact, the one who could not use the *dao* efficiently was rated as a woman and not allowed to enter into the *morung* (dormitory where bachelors used to sleep). Even at night, the men folk used to sleep with their *dao*-holder/cover which was moved from the back to the abdomen side while sleeping. Today, many people keep more than one case or holder well decorated and reserved for festive occasions.

All the Naga tribes have different types of *dao* case or holder but the Konyaks do not have a wooden one. They use a cane type which is shaped like a coil. The Southern Nagas like the Angamis, the Chakhesangs, and the Zeliangs; use small and round type *dao*-case. The Lothas, the Rengmas, and the Semas have the Ao type and they too use cowries and dyed goat hair. It is their custom to use such decorated items during feastive occasions. They considered this as one of the most important parts of the material cultures. The young generation need to learn how to make such things and they should carry on such cultural value from generation to generation.

1.10 The Casket

In the olden days of head hunting among the Nagas, every warrior had to plan means for thwarting the enemies who chased them. For this purpose, bamboo spikes were considered useful for they were sharply pointed at one end and they were fixed along the path of the attackers. About an inch from the pointed end, a ring is cut into the spike and as soon as the pointed head pierces any object, it breaks at the cut ring, making its removal even more difficult. To carry these spikes, the warrior require a special casket, a small conical basket *Sukhu* means carrier of spikes (Khu-basket, su or Asu-spikes). This casket have different names called by different tribes. The Aos call *'Chukhu,'* the Semas call it *Asaphu* and so on. There is a special type of basket *Sui-chukhu* in Ao dialect, which is used for special purposes. It has long bow tail type that resembles the horn of a *mithun.* That is why it is called *Sui-sukhu* (Su-Mithun), the Semas call it *Avikisaphu.*

Sui-Sukhu has two parts; the main basket and the tail; decorated with goat's hair and woman's hair. The basket is conical in shape, knitted with very fine bamboo or cane strips. The brim is decorated by providing a cover finely plated red cane and yellow orchid stalk. Also a fringe of red goat's hair about an inch wide runs along the brim of the basket. To this basket is attached the tail, (the horn like or bow like arched portion) and the top surface of this wooden tail is covered with that red and yellow plaited material using orchid stalks from both side and on the top of it is the goat's hair dyed red. Only towards the end of the tail a tuft of white goat's hair is used to enchance the contrast and beauty. Thus, white, black and red are the basic colours. The length of the goat's hair is only about a quarter of the human hair and the white and red portion are of equal length.

An inverted 'U' shaped, solid cane, is used to provide a handle to the basket, and this is fixed right to the bottom of the casket in the inner side. This handle is strong and allows the casket to be tied to the back of the man with the help of sash and put over the *dao* holder or *dao* case.

Sukhusa: In this, the long tail is absent and have only the basket with its handle. In addition, the tufts of goat's hair or the brimare is also absent but the human's hair are tied to the basket itself and the goat's hair of the same size as in the above type are attached on the top from the middle portion of the basket. Although, this is less attractive than the above type, it is preferred by the Nagas.

In the process of making such attire, the following steps are to be followed. (i) The materials are collected during the month of November to January; for, the wood cut during these seasons is free from insect infection, (ii) The tail attached in the first type involves inserting one portion of the curved stick into the basket and tying it firmly to the bottom of the basket and on the brim, (iii) A cane strip of the same width and length as the chosen piece of wooden tail has to be selected on which the hairs are tied on both the sides at regular but close intervals and this whole thing is then tied (even the nailed) to the wooden strip, (iv) The upper side of the tail is covered with woven strip of fine red cane and yellow skins or orchid stalk.

One may wonder as to how such long women's hair is obtained. During the head hunting days, the warrior who hunted the maiden's head was considered as double blessing because the head made him a hero whereas the hair added him another blessing to be used in such casket making. However, they never used the hair of those people who died of natural calamity.

It used to be more honourable to dance wearing a *Sukhu* with the hair of enemy. Infact, one was entitled to wear a *Sukhu* only when he hunted the head of an enemy. His sons could not inherit the right to wear it unless they had hunted a head too. *Sukhu* was, therefore, a dress exclusively of a real hero.

Generally, the Naga dresses give more prominence to the front side, but the back side of the body is left less decorated. But *Sukhu* is part of a dress which has to be put only in the backside of the body which gives more attraction and grand looking of a warrior or dancer.

Sukhu is used mainly by several Naga tribes. Among the Angamis, it is seldomly used though deserving old men are known to have used it on great occasions. The tribes of Tuensang, the Sangtam's, the Chang's, the Khiamngan's, the Yimchungers and the Phoms are very particular and their men folk never go to any festival without it. They all have their won names for it. The Konyaks of Mon district also use it.

It is regrettable that in the present generation with the event of modernization, some of these traditional dresses are disappearing, along with many other material cultures. There is an urgent need to make an attempt to make such ornaments not only for festive use but even for marketing exhibition outside the State. Now, there are every possibility to make such a valuable and costly items of Naga attire with the help of modern machines and make available in the world markets.

1.11 The Sash

In Ao language '*Chuku*' means basket of spikes, '*Mang*' means the body and '*ive*' means hanger. Literally, Chukumangive means the body hanger of casket i.e. the *Sash,* a long strip of cloth like belt worn around the waist for carrying the basket of spikes. Some dresses come only in pairs, and since, we have a basket there has to be the *Sash* that ties it also. The *Chuku* cannot be used without the *Sash* in festival dance. In other words *Chuku* is not complete without the *Sash.*

The Process of Making

First of all, one need to weave the cloth which is 4½ feet in length and about 9 inches in width. There are lose threads like laces on the two ends which are used for tying the basket. The main thread used is blue in colour, but red colour is used on the top for design. The *Sash* is folded longitudinally in the middle and one portion is concealed which is left plain blue, but the other visible portion has a design on the top. Almost 2½ feet of the central part has intersecting diagonal lines which create small rhombus shaped designs, and for this purpose red coloured thread is used. Even in the front visible portion, one and a half inch portion is left plain on the top of which the red dyed goat's hair are to be stitched in small bunches with yellow orchid tops. Below this, row of goat's hair; another row of longer bunches of goat's hair with five bunches of white goats hair in different four places are also stitched on the border of the *Sash.* The portion between the laces and the red designed in the middle is practically plain, except for a row of solid red rhombus on each side; setting apart the middle from the sides.

The cloth is woven by the wife of the warrior who has observed taboo (abstaining from sex) for atleast six days prior to the commencement of the task. An unmarried girl is not allowed to weave this *Sash.*

The man himself sets out to the jungle to collect the cane and the orchids stem, while the cane is easily obtainable. The yellow orchids stem is also fairly difficult to obtain. Often, the best orchids stem, grow on the branches of tall trees or high peaked cliffs and to get them is a challenging task. Infact, till the man returns from the forest, the family has to wait praying anxiously. His successful return from the jungle with the bundle of orchid stems is marked with happiness.

The orchid stems are cut into equal halves longitudinally and dried in the sunshine. After a month or so, the stem dry up completely and turns into gorgeous bright yellow colour. Now, these stumps are soaked in water to soften them so that the inner portion can be removed easily with the help of a sharp *dao.* The outer yellow skins, almost like a thin paper is then used for the ornamental works. For this, *job,* an adhesive is required and the indigenous gum or paste collected from the jungle is used. This paste will also be used for sticking the dyed red goats hair. The Aos call this special gum as '*kunem*' and it is collected out of wax and waste matter of the smallest bee *Menapetve.* The red dyed is prepared from materials like *Wali, Tangshi,* and *Tangmo.*

Before undertaking the dyeing of goats hair, the man should maintain purity abstaining from sex for six days and move into the jungle with all the things that he may require. Infact, this colouring/ dyeing is done secretly in total isolation. The area is fenced with branches of trees and a fire is lit in the centre on which the earthen pot is put. The ingredients (the collected chemical mentioned as above) are put into the water and into the boiling mixture, the goats hair are boiled for two hours or more. Automatically the red colour spreads and the hairs are dyed beautifully into a fast colour.

After collecting the dried stems of orchid plants and dyeing the goat's hair, bunches of goat's hair are prepared to be put on the *Sash.* In olden times, only a thin cane string and a *dao* was used while making the bunches. These are bent to create small 'U' shaped hooks, and the bunches of goats hair are tied to it. The orchid skins are small rectangle shaped pieces that are folded inwards along the breadth. A piece of thread is then passed through the folded portion with an inverted 'U' portion on the top and the bunch of goat's hair with the hooks intact is then put; and the orchid skin is gradually wrapped around it. The string passed through the fold is then pulled and knotted at the bottom, which becomes real insecurely tied as a result, is the bunch of a red hair with a beautifully yellow top and a small hook that can be stitched on the *Sash.*

Almost two or three hundred bunches may be required for each row depending upon the size of the man. It is thus, a fairly painstaking job and consumes several hours. While, the first row is only two inches in width, the parallel bottom row stitched on the margin of the *Sash* is of much longer bunches, nearly seven to eight inches in length. Once it is completed the entire thing looks more beautiful and is to be put over the shoulder and then the front side is also brought behind and tied to the other. This casket is hung over the *dao* case as described earlier.

This ornamental work is considered as one of the most beautiful attires for the man in Naga culture. This fine work is also allowed to wear only by those warriors who have succeeded in getting a head of the enemy.

Therefore, the man who wear such ornaments are highly honoured and respected in the society. Use of such ornaments is found to be common among the Nagas. In Sema, it is called *Amula kuva*, and the Khimngan's call it *Phacham*. The other tribes in Tuensang do use a shawl for the same purpose using two ends of one side for tying. The Angamis and the Chakhesangs do not use the red dyed goat's hair but have *Sashes* made of woollen or cotton threads with different design; infact, sometimes they use two numbers crossing each other.

These are priceless pieces of Naga culture and to buy them, one may have to spend as much as rupees two thousand five hundred for each. We must continue with such traditional items of material culture of our own even if the days of head hunting practices are over. Let it be a symbol of our beautiful cultural heritage in the days to come.

1.12 The Bell

The bell, *(Changtong)* is one of the part of Naga dresses which is made of brass metal. The Nagas were not known of such beautiful bell in the beginning. According to the story, it is said that such bell had been brought from Myanmar, China etc. It produces a beautiful sound just like the sound of musical instruments when we strike. However, it was not regarded as the musical instrument. Hence, instead of calling it as a musical instrument, it was used as a part of dress unlike other societies. The Nagas considered it as a sounding dress because it gives sound on movement. A man may wear as many dresses as he could; yet it is the bell that is ringing alongwith the movement of that person. That is why, it is known as sounding dress. It is not used by men alone but used for domestic animals like horse; cows etc. tied by the owners.

Every religion of the world has got its own pattern of worship. If we enter into a Hindu temple, there we can see a big bell hanging at the entrance of the hall. Without touching it, no one is allowed to go into the innermost sanctorum of the temple. Ringing of bell signifies that, God may hear that some people are coming to worship him. Similarly, one may find bell in every Christian churches throughout the world. As soon as the bell is rung, the believers use to go to the church and listen to the preaching of the word of God. Likewise, the bell is used for different purposes.

The Aos considered the bell as one of the most important ornaments both for men and women. Only the meritorious people are entitled to wear it especially the rich people. In a string, bells would be tied up atleast 12 to 14 in numbers at a distance of 5 to 6 inches. Now, the two ends of the string are tied together to make the shape of a long necklace. This is called bell necklace. This bell necklace is worn by many elderly women, of the wives of warriors or rich people during the time of national festival dance like *Moatsu* and *Tsungrem Mong.* Among the male dancers, only the heroes are entitled to wear this bell necklace. This bell necklace is called *Changtongzuk* in Ao dialect.

There are different types of dresses among the Nagas and bell is one of the most fashionable items for the Phom tribe of Tuensang district. The bell is tied hanging in the hips while dancing. Such an ornament is used by those people who are entitled to use it according to their custom. The womenfolk of Phoms are not allowed to wear the bell by customary law of the tribe. This bell is the ornament of the warriors only. Hence, it fits them nicely on any occasion. It is specially used during the time of *Aoling Mongyu* festival. They called it *Yamkong.* The Semas cannot ignore this beautiful bell as a dress. However, they rarely use this bell dress in their festival dances. They called it *Amugu.* However, the use of such bell as an ornament is not popular among other tribes except the Semas, the Aos, the Phoms and the Konyaks.

1.13 The Armlet

The Nagas are fond of covering different parts of the body with different fine ornaments. The wearing of armlet *Kumbang* is an example. The armlet is worn on their arms. They are of many kinds, made of different materials like elephant tusk, wood, iron, cane, bamboo etc. In the process of human civilization, man with his own creative efforts started ornamenting his body in order to add more attraction and beauty. The

Fig. 1.10 : The Casket

Fig. 1.11 : The Sash

Fig. 1.12 : The Bell

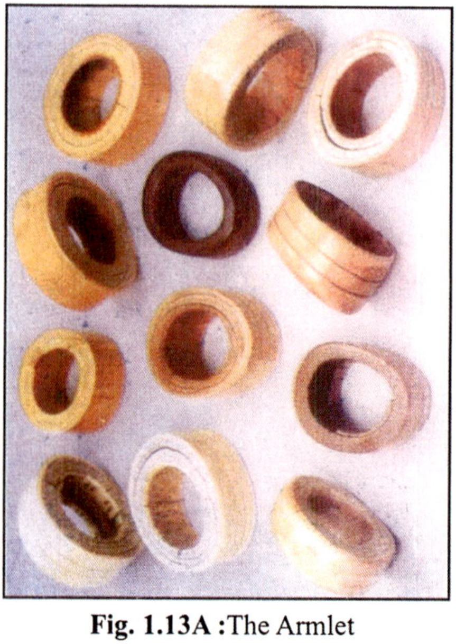

Fig. 1.13A : The Armlet

Fig. 1.13B : The Armlet

process of ornamenting mainly depends on three factors: (i) Availability of production inputs that are required to make ornaments such as materials, artisanship, craftsmanship and technology etc., (ii) The societal approval to be used as the ornaments of a particular type or by a particular community, (iii) Economic status of a group of people or individuals that could be afforded for a particular type of ornaments. The Nagas, in the olden times had also a desire to go for additional beauty. They adorned themselves with the ornaments which was manufactured with the help of indigenous technology. These ornaments are named differently in different tribal dialects; *Chietho* in Angami and *Akuhaghi* in Sema and so on.

In the past, the Naga forest was full of wild elephants. But now-a-days, due to rampant destruction of forest, the elephants are very rare except in some places like Wokha and Mon districts. It was very difficult to kill an elephant for men because there was no gun to shoot the elephant in those days. In the absence of gun, the Nagas used to kill the elephant by digging a big and deep pit in the path of the elephants. This pit is called '*Satiwangtsung*' in Ao dialect. The elephant would fall into such pit meticulously camouflaged by dried leaves. The fallen elephant was then killed by the villagers with missiles, stones, *daos,* spears etc. The tusks were then cut off with the help of axes and *daos*. The armlets were made out of these tusks. However, killing of elephant in Naga Country was banned later on by the British Government.

The process of making armlets is very interesting and difficult also. Many types of armlets are made out of ivory tusk. An armlet is also made out of wood, metal and cane. But the most important and costliest armlet is made of ivory. The width of the tusk is cut into sizes. Two parallel circular lines incurved round the armlet measuring 2 inches in between the lines on the outer surface are etched out. After completing the outer portion, a hole is then chiseled out in the centre of the armlet measuring 3 inches in width in the inner circle so that an arm can easily slip into the bicep. Finally, both the rims of the hole are smoothened on the sharp stones or other materials to avoid injury to the arms. In the absence of saw in the olden days, ordinary iron sick were used to cut the armlet and therefore, it took a lot of time for making a pair of armlets. The armlets were made only by the selected people after maintaining a period of purity for at least one week. If such formalities are not observed, it is believed that it may (the rim will) crack while cutting the armlet. Its longevity is good enough to have run even some hundred of years unless it is accidentally broken or burnt by fire.

According to the ancestors, armlets were imported from Bono and Mala, Borneo and Malaya. As Nagas are from South East Asia; the origin of such ornaments are believed to have brought from that side; and the people of those places might have supplied the relevant dresses and ornaments to the Nagas who left the original country. Moreover, the Angami traders brought armlets even from Culcutta, Mumbai, Chennai and Banaras and sold to other tribes of the Nagas especially by the Khonoma villagers. Every year, Khonoma traders came to Ao villages alongwith different types of traditional dresses for sale to the Aos. The entire Naga tribes wear armlet on all occasions. The armlet is entirely made of metal which is worn simultaneously with armlets made of ivory. These metal armlets are entirely for men.

The people of Tuensang district do not use only the ivory armlet but also armlet, made of cane fibre. The Khiamngans call it *Kiaplian* and the people of Sangtams call it *Rekhum*. The Konyaks use armlets of different shapes. The upper Konyaks use little thinner armlets with two strips in the middle; while the lower Konyaks use thicker armlets with different design engraved on them. They can be worn by the Ahngs the village chiefs. They can also be worn by the wealthy people and those who are noted for their valour and heroism. Among the Semas, the armlets are used by those who are wealthy and heroic. This is one of the sacred ornaments of men and hence, nobody can touch a man wearing armlets according to custom. The Semas wear these after promulgating such strict custom. Every Naga tribe use armlets but those armlets use by the Angamis, the Chakhesangs, the Aos and the Semas are considered to be the best and the costliest. The Zeliang people also use the same armlet.

In the olden days of Ao society, the armlets were not only used by the rich and heroic but also according to clanship and traditional social sanction. Like the Imchen's clan; who are the descendants of 'Tsungremchang' of the Mongsen group, now, living in different Ao villages can put on such armlets. According to practice, Anichar, Nungsangchar, Sor and Kichuchar were not entitled to wear it. Longkum and Pongen clans were entitled to put them on. The Jame clan, unless they were rich or empowered to sacrificial rites in the villages were not entitled to put it on. Such were the practices and beliefs among the Aos. However wearing of armlets in contemporary Naga society has no such restriction, especially during the festivals.

1.14 The Gauntlet

Another interesting item of the Naga attire is called *Khaup* in Ao. It is nothing but a gauntlet worn on the wrist glove. It is worn only by man. Gauntlet is being used for two different purposes. Firstly to make the arms strong, because a weak arm cannot perform any work especially in the battle field. Secondly, to deflect the enemies sword from attack. It is interesting to note the war tactics among the Nagas with bare *daos,* spear and the shield, in neck to neck situation. While fighting the battles against the enemy gauntlet was worn to make the arms stronger and to protect from the enemies weapon. These ornaments have been used by all the people of all countries at all times. Long before, the invention of the gun, fire arms and artillery, the nations of the world, mostly the Roman armies used these gauntlet made of metal. Moreover, many people of the world used these gauntlet even made of cloth also. The war lover Nagas, have been using this item from times immemorial, not only as a weapon but as ornaments too.

The Nagas regarded this gauntlet as one of the best and most favourite ornaments to wear on certain festive occasions. The Angamis, the Chakhesangs, the Zeiliangs etc. do wear the gauntlet woven with yarns of different colours. Normally, it is entirly a male dress. The Naga custom and tradition prohibits wearing of such gauntlet by women, but on festive occasion they use bangles and bracelets. The Aos, the Semas, the Lothas, the Rengmas etc. use special type of gauntlet which is more attractive. The Semas call it *Awukukha.* It is being used in plenty by the people of Tuensang and Mon districts of Nagaland. The Khiamngans call it *Pha-khon.*

The process of making gauntlet is rather simple. A small piece of cloth may also be used for the purpose. A small piece of bamboo is inserted in both the ends longitudinally. After this cowries are stitched up in line by line. These cowries are hard shells obtained from marine animals of the ocean. These are available in plenty near the Andaman and Nicobar Islands, and in the islands of South East Asia etc.

First of all, the belly and the two sides are pressed out in stones and thus stitched in the cloth which is ready for this purpose. Simply stitching cowries do not make a gauntlet perfectly. A thick fringe of dyed goat's hair is also attached to make the gauntlet perfect and beautiful. For this, three cane fabrics and adhesive which is called *Konem* in Ao dialect are needed. With the help of these materials, one can make the beautiful fringe of red goat's hair and these are put in the larger side of the cloth for both hands. This red decoration is called

Olukobang in Ao dialect adding more beautiful and grand looking.

The gauntlet is one of the best ornamental dresses used by all the Naga tribes. However it can be worn by the heroes. All who are qualified to wear can do so not only on festive occasions but in all times, if he feels to do so. A man wearing such an ornament with decorated spear in his hand looks more grand and attractive. With this, he really looks like a hero of the land.

1.15 The Naga Spear

The Naga spears are of different types and usages:

(i) *Head hunting spear:* It was used only during the war of head hunting.
(ii) *Animal hunting spear:* It is known as hunting spear used during the hunting of wild animals.
(iii) *Festive spears:* This type of spear is used during festival only.
(iv) *Common spear* (unrestricted one): This can be used any time by any person without restriction.

The handle of the Naga spear is made of Nahor/palm tree (iron wood) and oak tree with an approximate length of five to seven feet, used for different purposes as mentioned above. Now-a-days, more beautiful decorated spears of different sizes are coming out even for marketing purposes. The warrior during any encounter speared the enemies and took the heads of the slained persons to the village with great triumph. Such spears were sanctified and kept for future use. Unfortunate warriors were often killed and likewise their heads were taken by the enemies. The spear used by the warrior was known as 'Man hunting spear'. This particular spear could not be used for any other purpose.

Story tells us that men were killed by wild animals during rainy seasons. Even today, we see dead bodies of men being killed by wild animals with our own eyes. The people of Ao tribe and the clan who are authorised by tradition used to give offerings in such an occasion. The entire villagers are banned from going to the jungle on that day. During such times, any outsider who happens to be in the village is allowed to witness the mass hunting of the tiger. However, there it is cautioned that such person while witnessing the hunting, should stand with their close friends as a means of protection/shelter because it is presumed that the tiger use to attack the outsiders or the weak persons on the pretext that he is inferior than the others.

Otherwise, such person should remain in the village with the sentry or watchmen of the village. On completion of such hunting, the outsiders are set free and sent to their respective villages. On cush occasions, only the particular spears which are preserved after proper sanctification are used for this purpose.

Wildboars are of two types known as *Pongi Saja* and male boar normally roams alone. The other type of wildboar is known as *Pongi Salu* which means in a group with a leader of the group. This type of wildboar normally live in group around 50 to 60 boars. Such type of wildboars move around mainly during summer and autumn seasons. It is very interesting to watch such group from a distance. They thus destroy the paddy and other plantation in the field. On such occasion, the villagers undertake a mass hunting in a planned manner without fear as a part of festival. They are perfectly trained to attack such wild animals with spear and *dao,* and kill them.

Wildboar meat is good for human consumption, when the wildboar is killed, the meat is cut into many pieces and divided among the villagers as per traditional norms. The spear which is specially sanctified and preserved for this purpose is used in such occasions only. This spear is known as 'Wildlife hunting spear'. Such spear shall not be used for any other purpose.

The Naga festival spear is such a beautiful one. It is more decorative and attractive. The rich and the warrior can use more attractive and decorative spear than the common people by tradition. Thus, a person can use any type of spear depending on the status of the person by tradition and customs. On the other hand, a person is not authorised by norms to use a spear of any kind above his status. However, it is relaxed to use any kind during the traditional festivals. This traditional norms are still in practice by the Nagas since times immemorial.

Different Naga tribes have different types of festivals and dances. The type of dance where *dao,* spear and shield are used is known as *Jilupentem* or war dance. The dance performed with full traditional dresses in lines in known as *Sangpangtsu* dance. The *Jilupentem* and *Sangpangtsu* dances are very interesting to witness. Similarly dances are performed by both women and men folk, though tradition do not permit the women folks to perform and dance with *dao,* spear and shield. However, the Ao women can hold a *dao* while performing dance. Such spears which are used during dances are known as festival spears. The word festival here we mean, a traditional festival. Prayer is offered to God of the Sun and the Moon to grant long life during traditional festivals and add more blessings. Therefore, on this special festivals, various types of spears which are especially designed and well decorated for such purposes with red dyed goats hair are used meaningfully.

The Common Spear or unrestricted spear can be used for any purpose. This spear can be used for various purposes e.g. travelling, funeral, function, traditional offerings to God in the field, domestic purposes, fishing and collection of vegetables from the forest. This type of spear can be sold to others too, except the first-three ones. The first two type of Naga spear i.e. the man hunting spear and the wildlife hunting spear are not commonly used today because the days of head hunting period is no more and wild animals are also no more available; moreover guns are used instead of spear.

The decorated Naga Spears have attracted tourists and other visitors to Nagaland. They like to keep them as decorative piece. Such decorated spears are now available in different sizes even with stand to hold it and keep at home. The Naga craftsmen are now manufacturing most beautiful spears in huge numbers and sending outside the state. This is a good trend of cultural diffusion.

1.16 The Naga Dao

Different people of different countries use different types of *dao* for various purposes. Since the Nagas are closely attached to the nature around them; *dao* is regarded as the most important weapon. This is the main tool being used by the Nagas even today for earning their livelihood.

They use different types of *dao*. Some tribes use small and crooked ones, while others use long and larger *daos*. Large and long *daos* are used by most of the Nagas. The Nagas regard their *daos* as one of the most important equipments because it serves many purposes for their survival. Therefore, *dao* is termed as saver and loser of life too. Because it saved many lives and killed many lives too in the past.

One can notice that four types of *daos* are used for four different purposes in Naga society as in the case of spear. They are:

1. Head hunting *dao*
2. Animal hunting *dao*
3. Working *dao*
4. Ceremonial *dao*.

During the days of head hunting period, nobody could predict as to when and from which direction the enemies would came. Therefore, a given age group of men were always kept ready with the war equipments to fight with their enemies. The adult male members of the family were ever alert with weapons, such as, *dao,* spear, war shield (bamboo shield) and spikes (aso), or bows and arrows. Military war tactics and training was given in *Arju,* the bachelors dormitory where the bachelors used to sleep together with *dao* and spear. When the head of the enemy was brought to the village, *dao* was sanctified again. The *dao* with which the head of enemies were cut is known as Head hunting *dao.*

In the same manner, the *dao* by which the wild animals were killed was also sanctified before they were preserved for future use. During the days of head hunting, one could not go freely for fishing and hunting, except in groups because of the fear of enemies. The wildboar and tiger which normally live in deep and ghostly forest happened to pass through the villages and thereby attacked the people suddenly causing to death. On such occasions, the whole villagers used to attack the ferocious wild animal by using the sanctified *dao,* spear and shield. Later, those weapons were again sanctified and kept for future use. However, such weapons are not used for other activities.

The Nagas are fond of eating meat of wildboar and as such the entire villagers used to surround the particular forest with bamboo and wood fencing where such animals live and thereby, such animals were killed with *dao* and spear. On such a occasion, all the adult male members of the village used to do the fencing works in the jungle and chase the animals; while women folk prepared food and drinks to cheer up the menfolk engaged in attacking the wild animals. This is one of the most fascinating games practised by the Nagas. Killing of a tiger and exhibition of its death body is another interesting thing. Whenever a tiger is killed, the mouth of the tiger is kept widely opened with a piece of stick *Tangmosung* and the ear is tightly closed with a kind of leaves called *Pangsemo.* It is then kept on a platform to exhibit to the community. Such exhibition is arranged mainly in a road junction where everyone could see it. In certain villages having two *khels;* the whole body of the tiger is kept over the bamboo made structure in a good location where the travellers could see it from a far. A bundle of wooden and bamboo missiles are also kept in place of *dao* and spear in the surrounding areas in order to proof that the tiger was actually killed with *dao* and other such sharp weapons. It is believed that other tigers use to visit the place at night where the dead body of the tiger is kept. Then they mourn bitterly counting the number of the weapons uttering the following words cursing the killers. "Tongkü - one. Tongnü - two. Tongsen - three. Tongeli - four. Tongpanga - five. Tongterok-six. Tongteni - Seven. Tongtsuet - Eight. Tongtükü - Nine. Tongtera - Ten etc."

The tiger's meat is generally considered as an evil spirited one therefore it is not eatable. The *dao,* the spear and the shield by which the tiger is killed are then sanctified and preserved for future use. Such daos are known as *Kiyi, Pongzu alepa Nok*; which means, the *dao* which kill the tiger and wild boar.

The Nagas earned their livelihood with *dao* as modern men earn their livings by machines. A Naga family cannot survive without *dao* even today and most of the works are done with the help of *dao.* Therefore several number of *daos* are kept at every home for each member of the family. This *dao* is known as the 'working *dao'*. That is the *dao* which earns their livelihood. The Nagas use to keep different types of such working *daos* for different kinds of work at home, in the field and in the jungle.

The last one is known as the 'Ceremonial *dao'*. In every festival only sanctified ceremonial *daos* are used as a traditional custom. The tribes hail from Tuensang district use the largest and longest daos while dancing. Thus, they look more grand and smart exhibiting the real Nagas. Such *daos* are not used as working *dao.* They are beautifully decorated with cane rings and colourful animals' hairs. This is a part of Naga culture with its distinctive-ness.

1.17 The Men's Shawl

Nagaland is land of beautiful and diversified shawls. They wear different types of colourful shawl. Different tribes have different types of shawl both for male and female. They all have different designs and colours indicating different meanings. If one looks at the Nagaland Calendar of 1997, published by the Government of Nagaland, Department of Publicity and Information, he will find almost all the major shawls worn by the Nagas. The followings are some of the popular shawls of different tribes worn by male only.

One of the popular shawls of the Aos is called *Mangkoteptsü* (head painted shawl). By tradition this is a shawl which is not entitled to be worn even by all male members. In the past only the rich man and warriors were entitled to wear this shawl. This is a status symbol shawl. Rich man could wear it by virtue of the *mithun* feast offered to

Fig. 1.14 : The Gauntlet

Fig. 1.15A : The Naga Spear

Fig. 1.15B : The Naga Spear

Fig. 1.16 : The Naga Dao

the community. The warriors are also entitled to wear this shawl because of their bravery demonstrated in head hunting practice. This shawl has rich cultural meanings. It is also called *Tsüngkotepsü* which is nothing but *Mangkotepsü* painted with *Tangkotzü*, a kind of design; obtained from *Tangko* tree, which is commonly available in Ao region.

Mangkotepsü is a striped cloth of red and black. It is composed of three pieces, joint together as a complete shawl. There are five big red stripes followed by the small red stripes on one segment. Another same piece of cloth with five thin black stripes is made which is about five inches in width on which different pictures depicting human head, *chaplee,* (ancient currency, lion, tiger, elephant, and cock etc.) are painted.

Five big red stripes represent woman's number given by God, that means women's number is five. The white piece at the middle pictures are painted with black which signifies men's number which is more than women by one. It means to say that women's number is 5 (five) whereas the men's number is 6 (six) according to Aos' beliefs. Women's number will be outside and the men's number which is in the middle. When these three pieces are stitched together, it becomes a ready made shawl. This shawl is considered the most honoured shawl of the Aos. Unlike other ordinary shawls *Mangkotepsü* cannot be worn by the ordinary people, for it is worn only by those who are meritorious and successful warriors. In other words, it is only a warrior's shawl or a rich man's shawl.

The most popular shawl of the Konyaks is called *Shotsü*. This is particularly worn by rich man. The *Angh* and the village elders too have a separate shawl known as *Metsü*. Today one may see different types of shawl both for males and females. The Konyak youngsters have developed a shawl popularly known as 'Konyaks uniform'. This is a striped cloth of red and black. Within a span of few years, the Konyak Nagas developed themselves into weaving and making shawls of different types and designs.

The Lotha Men's shawl is called *Longpensü*. This shawl is also striped with blue and black colours with green borders at both the ends. It is made in two separate pieces and later stitched together. In the middle, four stripes of about 2 inches, and two blue stripes of about 1 inch size is put lengthwise. In the blue stripes not very prominent pictures are put here and there with red colour. And in the margins, another design is woven with yellow and red colour. This shawl is not colourful one unlike many other tribal shawls. This shawl is also worn by rich men and warriors only.

The Semas, too have separate shawls for both males and females. One particular shawl known as *Apuasugheemi* is worn by menfolks only. It is woven all in black with four stripes in red about 1 inch at both the ends of the shawl. Both the borders are in red where beautiful zigzag patterns are woven in red, green and white. At both the ends the remaining thread laces are decoratively bound together with green colours. In the middle, pictures are woven in a row of the lines in red.

All tribes in Tuensang district have their own distinctive shawls. Each tribe has separate shawls for both men and women. These are worn specially during festivals adding more glamour and appealing of its design with rich colours. One particular shawl is worn by many tribes today, i.e. the Chang shawl. This shawl is made of most colourful threads like black, red and blue. There are five blue stripe lines about four inches in breadth and the other piece of the same cloth of the same size striped in red colour about 6 inches in breadth are woven in between the blue lines. In each blue line, square patterns in red are put. And, in the largest blue line, zigzag pattern is put with red and blue threads alternately. If both the zigzag ends, ended downward, it is considered as a good sign. And, if one end is ended upward it is considered as a bad sign. Therefore, it is required to be careful while selecting such beautiful Chang shawl which has become a common shawl of the Nagas today.

The Angamis of Kohima district has two typical shawls in white and in black. The white shawl is called *Loramboushu*. This shawl is woven in white and in the middle, designs are woven with black and red about 6 inches in length and 3 inches in breadth. The other shawl is black with stripe lines of three in red and green about half inch in breadth. Nice designs are put at one end of the shawl. This shawl is known as *Lohi*. In both the shawls, extra unwoven threads are hanging which are uniformly maintained at one end. This end is beautifully stitched that one can hardly observe that it is done with a needle. Both the shawls are worn by both males and females.

Among the Rengmas, both men and women have separate shawls. Most of their shawls are very decorative and colourful. One particular men's shawl is known as *Anutsu*. This shawl is woven separately in small sizes. Firstly, five black pieces and four white about two inches width are made and small designs are put in the white portions. In between each black, pictures in red and black are put together. All these pieces when stitched together makes a complete shawl of the Rengmas.

The Chakhesangs too have separate shawls for both males and

females. They have a particular shawl called *Thipikhu.* In this shawl, typical pictures like elephant, *mithun,* flowers etc., are put in red, white and green colours. Another type of shawl used by menfolks is a combination of many colours. For example, white, black, red and blue colours are put together in a row in four separate pieces. All these are woven by thread. Later, these four pieces are joint together and stitched with red and blue colours. They are joint in such a way that all the white portions are in one place where it is being stitched. This shawl is called *Samakhu.* The Zeliang shawls are more or less similar to that of the Angamis in various ways.

Thus, each Naga tribe has distinctive shawls for both males and females. These are very beautiful and warm shawls. They are liked by many people of the world today, and these beautiful Naga shawls have great scope in the world market today.

1.18 The Leggings

Leggings are another ornamental dress of the Nagas worn by males on special occasion of festivity. It is worn between the ankles and knees as leg gloves. Leggings are generally worn in pair like shoes. It is about one foot in length and has two ends, upper and lower. The circumference is about 14 inches. The middle portion has its circumference of 17 inches in size.

This beautiful ornamental dress can be made only by a few persons. According to their beliefs and practice, the man who make such items must also refrain from sex atleast for certain period of time. As a general rule, younger persons were not allowed to make this item, because of the fact that they cannot refrain from absolute sexual abstinence. The makers of such item were not allowed to participate in any funeral function of a dead person during the process of making.

Different materials are required to make leggings. They are white and red cane fibres and yellow skin of orchid. Cane is a free gift of nature which can meet many requirements of mankind. It is cut into thin slices and are dyed in red colours. They yellow skin of the orchid is obtained from the branches of big trees in the forest and dried in sunshine. The lower part of the leggings which is about 6 inches long is made completely with white cane fibre. At the same time all the white canes are replaced or joined by red cane fibres and metted upto 6 inches long with a mixture of yellow orchid skin making a diagonal design. After this, the whole white portion is cut into or opened at one side longitudinally just to let the legs put easily and wear it conveniently.

On the cut portion, two small bamboo sticks are put and tied in one corner of the opening, and leave it hang freely. This string is used as a locker. To make the leggings more beautiful, three pieces of thick round laces are attached to one of the sticks in three places. Making of leggings is a difficult job, and it requires months together to complete a pair of leggings accurately.

The leggings are a part of ceremonial dress and they are normally worn on special occasion. When the dancers show the uniform movement by wearing them, it really looks so grand. The uniform movement of the legs is known as *Jangkang* or *Jangyu* in Ao dialect. Except a few of the Naga tribes, leggings are common to all. The Zeliangs apply a kind of paste, made of chewed rice water on their legs instead of using leggings while dancing. And that can be washed after the dance is over. The same is repeated in the next day.

Again, the people of Tuensang district like the Changs, the Phoms, the Yimchungers, the Sangtams, and the Khiamngans make their leggings mostly from bear's skin. When the bear is killed, the skin is removed carefully and dried in the sun for several days; and then it is cut according to the size of the legs and make their leggings. The Naga dances look more majestic when hundred of young men wearing leggings dance, making thunderous sound and earth shaking stomping of foot. The Khiamngans call the leggings *Hokon*. The Lothas use both cane and cotton made leggings, of which cotton made leggings are more popular. The Konyaks are fond of such ornament as the Rengmas. This is their favourite dress during festival. The Sangtams also wear this dress in great favour. They call it *Jingshi* in their dialect.

There is a particular custom among the Aos, the Angamis, the Semas and the Chakhesangs that they do not use bear's skin leggings. They use leggings made of cane fibres, both white and red, with yellow skin or orchid stem with beautiful design and patterns. The most favourite dress of the Aos are leggings. They wear it in all the dances and also while performing rituals to the moon and the sun during *Moatsu* and *Tsungrem-mong*. This dress is called *Jangta* in Ao dialect. The Semas also use such beautiful leggings while dancing. They call it *Apukhukukha*. This is very common among the Chakhesangs of Phek district too. All the men folk wear it in their *Tsukhoyie* festival days as their tradition.

Again, the Angamis have the same leggings known as *Phipa*. They always wear it during festival like *Sekrenyie*. In olden days, Khonoma villagers were the main manufacturers of such leggings. The Angami traders came to Ao region to sell leggings there. The people of

Angamis and Chakhesangs use leggings alongwith black cane fibre known as *Phiso*. When the Khonoma traders came to Ao region during olden times, they used to wear *Phipa* and *Phiso* with great charms. Such beautiful Naga culture dress can also be promoted making the Naga culture more unique in the process of cultural diffusion in this beautiful world of culture.

1.19 The Naga Shield

In this article, an attempt has been made to describe the Naga Shield with reference to its classification, design and process of making. The shield was considered as one of the most important weapon used during the days of traditional Naga society. It was used for different purposes as described below.

Design and Techniques of Making

According to types, there are (i) Bamboo made shield and (ii) leather shield. Design and production techniques are differently used in both the types of such shield. Bamboo made shield has three main components namely the frames, the body and the handle. The major items used in bamboo shield are the cane and the bamboo. The process begins with making of frame outlining the border of the shield. For this purpose, a long and strong cane stick of around one inch in diameter is longitudinally split into two equal halves and bent in an inverted 'U' shape so that the frame has two long parallel sides and a semicircular top. The base of the shield is also bounded with equally strong cane of equal diameter (longitudinally split into two halves) in such a way that it remains in an arc shape, being concave towards the line joining the open ends of the inverted ('U') shaped frame and convex towards outside. The main body of the bamboo shield is tightly woven with bamboo splits. The bamboo used for weaving the shield is of a special type called *Jangpo* in Ao dialect which is very strong and sticky. Other ordinary bamboos being weak fibres and insect prone, are not used for such purpose. This special quality bamboo is brought from the forest in the month of November and December, i.e. just after the winter months starts. The materials are kept under the sun for few days in order to season it properly. After the bamboo is fully seasoned, it is spilt into several pieces with the help of a sharp *dao* for making bamboo smoother splints are to be used in weaving process.

The bamboo used for making the shield is quite different from that of the basket weaving. For this purpose, only the outer skin of the bamboo is used. The bamboo piece is made thinner from the inner side. In the outer face of the splint, only the model outgrowth is smoothened. The bamboo's thickness of the splint used in shield making is around 5 to 6 mm which is greater than that of the splints used for an ordinary basket. While processing bamboo splint into splints, a portion in the prism shape is left in the inner middle part, and this distinguishes the splints into two such as:

(i) The splints with longer prism (of around 4 cm height) and (ii) The splints with shorter prism (of around 1½ cm height). The thickness of the splint which is uniform throughout its length (other than the prism portion) is regulated by the manipulation of hand. While smoothening, the inner side of the bamboo splint, the bamboo stick is kept on the left hand and the sharp *dao* in the right. The cutting edge of the blade of the *dao* is kept pressed against the stick at a point to be one of the ends of the prism while the forefinger is kept beneath the stick below the *dao* for having control over the process. Now, the splint is drawn inward with the help of the left hand while the *dao* is kept pressed on to the splint and pushed outward with the right thumb. This is repeated several times till the same part of the splint is smothened and ready to be woven. The same process is again repeated for the other end of the splint by putting the *dao* blade on the point to be the other end of the prism. Care is taken to see that the thickness of the bamboo splint covering the prism is not reduced and the prism remains without any crack or damage.

The next step is weaving or knitting of the body of the shield. The splints with longer and shorter prisms are alternatively arranged on the floor in a series, and then, splint (Alternatively with longer and shorter prisms) are plaited in a definite technique called 'twilled design' (each splint to be plaited passes over and then by making an angle of 45° with two splints arranged on the floor). But in the middle point, little deviation takes place. It is designed that two adjoining splints (warps) are over or under the two adjoining (wefts). This is done by reducing the jump by one splint of the warps alternatively. Just two splints before the middle line of the body of the shield. While weaving, the outer skin of the bamboo is always exposed outside and the prisms are systematically arranged to form the backbone of the shield. All the longer prisms are supported with two shorter prisms, one adjacent to the upper half at the right side and the other adjacent to the lower half at the left side. All the prisms meet each other forming a right angle.

The knitted body of the shield is then longitudinally curved with the help of a circular wooden log with a view to make the shield convex towards the enemies. This convex shield protects the warrior in a better way against the incoming spear attack. The spear heads coming with a perpendicular force cannot easily pierce because of the strong backbone made of the prisms as discussed above and the spearheads with an inclined force coming from another angle also cannot easily pierce because of the smooth and sticky convex face of the shield. Then, the woven body is bordered by clamping the inverted 'U' shaped frames on both the sides and stitching circularly by thin cane threads at a distance of around 2 to 3 inches throughout the border. The stitching is performed by close spiral movement of the cane thread, at least 5 to 6 times on a particular spots of stitching.

The handle is 'H' shaped and made of three strong bamboo sticks; two of the sizes being 6 inches and one of the size around 4 inches. All these bamboo sticks are wrapped completely with thin and fine cane splints in order to have a grip control on it, otherwise, the bare bamboo sticks become slippery. The 'H' shaped handle is fixed in the middle part of the shield in a convenient way both horizontally and vertically. The handle is further supported by a shoulder belt, simply a chord, made of thin cane splints in order to have hold on the shield and to save from slips and grip. The shoulder belt helps the warriors to bring the shield to the usual grip and without losing concentration towards the enemies. The height of shield and the place on which the handle is fixed depends upon the height of the user. Normally, it is designed to cover the whole body from the neck to the knee of a person.

The leather shield is made of either buffalo or *mithun* skin. The skin of a grown up buffalo or *mithun* is then taken out and dried under the sun for several days particularly during the winter months. This season is preferred in order to avoid decay of the skin due to moisture in the atmosphere in other seasons. A circular wooden log (normally a log of cotton tree because of its softness) is chosen to fix the skin, spread over it and nailed with bamboo spikes. The skin is kept under the sun till it is completely dried up. Then, with the help of a sharp *dao* the leather is cut into required size. The longitudinal sizes in a straight line horizontal to the ground; and the top straight towards outside. When the leather is taken out of the circular log, it becomes longitudinally convex to outside the concave towards the user. The 'H' shaped handle, in the same way as discussed in case of bamboo shield is fixed in the inner middle part of the shield. The handle is again supported with a shoulder belt.

The leather shield is heavier than the bamboo shield and cheaper also. The leather shield is less preferred for war purpose, however, it is often used during festival dance after drawing some designs on its face. The Angamis sometimes border their leather shield with the help of cane splints and the process of bordering is not so similar to that of the bamboo shield.

SOCIO-CULTURAL BELIEFS ASSOCIATED WITH SHIELD MAKING

The production of Naga shield is not only confined to the materials, mechanical design and the technology used in it. But some socio-cultural formalities are mandatorily observed in the process of making a shield. The time of material collection is followed by a *Kimo* in Ao dialect, which means the period when purity is maintained. The *Kimo* period is longer atleast for seven days before the collection of required materials. This period puts some restrictions on the maker and family members also, such as not to eat anything in other's house or outside, not to visit any house where a death has occurred, not to sleep with his wife, not to allow his sons and daughters to go to the dormitory of the village etc. During the first-three days, all the above purity measures are strictly followed in the family. After the purity period is over i.e. on the eight day or onwards, the maker of the shield starts collecting all the relevant materials from the forest. Usually, the maker smoothens the outer mode of the bamboo before or after making the bamboo slits. He then makes the shield carefully to avoid eventualities. After the shield is completed, it is examined by the village witchcraft. If any knot or node is left unsmoothened or any outgrowth is found on the face of the shield, it is not used for the main purpose for which it is designed. In such a case, the maker engages a wage earner and ask him to throw it in the graveyard of the village. Then he is given a small remuneration for the job; may be some rice or common salt. It is believed that the shield with any out growth or unsmoothened face or unsmoothened bamboo node is unauspicious and invites death of the users in a warfield or shortens the life span of the user or maker himself. This was the belief involved in shield making.

Even among the Nagas, some section of people do not eat the meat of *mithun* or buffalo or cow. Such uneaten animal's skin are not used for making the shield. It is believed that those who violates such practices his longivity is shortened or face danger in a warfield.

Another important social taboo associated with shield making is the restriction of the children to make such an item because of their immaturity and inconsistency. It suggests that the shield is made with perfection and without violating any norm or social belief associated with it. It is understood that the children cannot perform the whole process without a mistake such as following the taboo and the pattern of weaving the splints in their perfect order smoothening the splints accurately. Thus, as per the social customs, the children should not be given the task of making a shield, which has importance in protecting human life against several dangers and hazards. This social taboo explains the importance of Naga shield and the seriousness involved in its making process. Those warriors, who do not know how to make it or those who are not skillful enough to design in a proper way, usually purchase it from others for their own use.

FUNCTIONAL CLASSIFICATION

The Naga shield, as a protective weapon is used in different ways depending upon the nature and type of enemies, such as enemy in a warfield, fire protection, wild beasts, particularly the tiger and wild boar etc. From the functional point of view, shield is classified into four categories; each category has its own characteristics, methodology of use, and governing rules as stated below:

(i) War Shield

While fighting with the enemies, shield is used as a protective device to save his life from the attack. In a traditional war, the commonly used weapons are the *dao,* the spear and the bow and the arrow. The shield, being a long and wide object, can protect the life. Sometimes, the shield falls short of length to cover the whole body of a warrior; and in such a situation, the shield user moves the shield quickly towards the direction of attacking weapon and hides behind the shield.

The traditional warriors in other societies of India, such as the people of Assam, the Daiks of Orissa, Rajputs and the soldiers of Mughal India also used shield in the warfield but their shield were small, round and oval shaped made of metals specially designed to protect from the sword.

In contrast to those shields, the Naga shield is made from non-metallic objects and of longer size and tailor made because the Naga way of fighting is different. Before using the shield in a war, it is first sprinkled with water to make it more slippery and sticky. After the war is over, the shield is sanctified once again by worshipping and is kept hanging in its own place i.e. nearer to the fire place so that it gets kitchen smoke and soot for enchancing its durability. The process of sanctification signifies the stoppage of war and restoring of peace and the war shield should not be used till there is another war called in the land.

(ii) Tiger Shield

The Naga villages were surrounded with dense forest, full of wild animals. Sometimes wild animals particularly the tigers entered into the villages and caused harm to the villagers either by killing persons or their domestic animals. This was a regular happening in almost all the Naga villages. The Naga villagers, therefore, used to attack the tiger with shield and other weapons. They first chased the tiger into the jungle and start searching for the place where it takes shelter. Once the tiger's cage or shelter is located, it is guarded by people from every side. They then check all possible exits with the help of strong bamboo and wood fencing. Such fencing is known as *Akuchi* in Ao dialect. After the broad strong fencing is over, the adult male members enter inside the fencing with their traditional weapons such as *dao*, spear and shield. At the time of entering inside the fence and approaching towards the tiger they shout with loud voices in order to terrify the tiger. The tiger becomes more wild and furious and start attacking the people. The group attacks the tiger protecting themselves with the shield from the attack of the tiger. Neither the tiger nails nor the teeth can touch the hunter when he protects himself behind the shield. In the process, one hand holds the shield protecting the body and other hand holds the *dao* or spear to attack the tiger. The war takes place till the tiger is killed; and in the process, the shield performs two functions, i.e. protection of the body and creation of terrifying sound due to its structure and design. Immediately, after use, the shield is sanctified and hanged in its usual place till it is needed for the same purpose. Since this shield is exclusively used for fighting against the tiger; it is called 'Tiger shield'.

(iii) Dance Shield

The dance shield is sometimes called as "festival shield" exclusively used for dance purpose, particularly on the occasion of important festivals. The dance shield is usually shorter than the war shield and the tiger shield. The shield designed and made for the purpose of dance is decorated further on its front side. Lines are drawn from the mid-point of the nasal line, those encurved at the top with a view to giving a flower like structure. This artistic work is performed with the help of either charcoal or burnt animal bones or limestones. At the ends of both the parallel sides of a dance shield, a bunch of red coloured goat hair called *Jongpen* in Ao dialect is fixed to add to the beauty of the object. The use of *Jongpen* also signifies the status of a dancer. The dancers move to their respective shield in rhythm and in tune with the background music with drum sound leading the dancers. Through their dance and songs, the dancing male members convey the women group how bravely they fight in a warfield. In the process of their musical message, they demonstrate their war story in a dancing form, and the act of demonstration involves the use of shield, *dao,* spear and other weapons. Since the women do not go to the warfield, they come to know through this dance and song how warriors fight and kill their enemies in a warfield. During the interval of the dance programme they keep the shield vertically either with the help of an external support and perform some sports activities by jumping forward over the successive shield like a hurdle race. When the dance is over, the shield is again sanctified and kept preserved on its original place till the next dance occasion comes.

(iv) Common Shield

The common shield is used for other purpose unlike the three mentioned above and there is no restriction in its use nor it requires any sanctification after it is used for any particular purpose. This shield unlike the other three mentioned above can be used by any person including the children. The two most common uses of this shield are, fire control and children game. In the olden days, when the Nagas were living in thatched houses fire was frequently breaking out and in the process of fire fighting, they used such shield. When the fire continues to spread from one house to another, the control device adopted by the Nagas is to demolish one or two houses ahead of the affected houses so that the flow of fire is controlled. While breaking the house it is difficult to stand at the spot because of high temperature and blowing of hot wind. In such a situation the common shield is used as a protective device particularly to protect the person against hot wind. While one of his hand holds the shield, the other hand is busy with a *dao* or axe, cutting the bamboo and wooden pillars of the house to be demolished.

Sometimes fire breaks out in the jungle which needs immediate control. There also the common shield is used as a protective device. Apart from the use in fire fighting, the common shield is also used as a weapon while war training is imparted to the children. Since the war shield, tiger and the dance shield are all restricted ones, the trainer asks the trainees to bring the common shields for demonstration. Since the structure and size of the common shield is similar to the war shield, it acts as a substitute of the war shield for the purpose of training. With the help of this, the trainer demonstrates how they (trainees) are to use different types of shield for different purposes.

The common shield unlike the other shields can be sold out to any person. But the first-two shields cannot be sold out.

The functional classification of Naga shield thus tells about the different uses and the importance assigned to each type of the shield. The first-three categories of shields are very important and a lot of social importance is attached to them. The norms of their use are strictly followed as a common practice in Naga society.

The shield was an indispensable weapon in traditional Naga society which performed different functions. The shape, the design and the patterns of knitting a Naga shield with simple bamboo splits and canes exhibits an interesting artistic talents and indigenous wisdom of the Nagas.

Fig. 1.17A : The Men's Shawl

Fig. 1.17B : The Men's Shawl

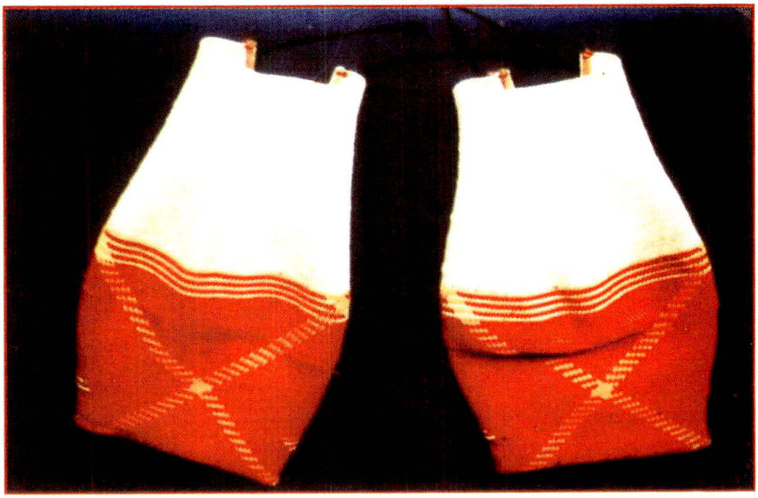

Fig. 1.18 : The Leggings

Fig. 1.19 : The Naga Shield

2

THE WOMEN'S ATTIRE

2.1 The Brass Hair Band

The Nagas are very fond of festivals and merry making. In such festivals, people of every tribe, both men and women use to put different kinds of dresses. As in other societies, the Naga women keep their hairs intact, and use a kind of hair band which is called 'Brasshair band'. It is made up of brass metal. Story tells us that this materials was brought from 'Mann' country which is called Myanmar at present, the last country which the Naga people had come across during the early centuries.

In order to wear a brass ear-ring, both ears are to be pierced at the upper and the lower ear lobes at the early age. The parents strictly maintain the purity till the wounds of the ears are completely healed. A coiled brass rod as big as half an inch round which is coiled three times and is put in the holes. Its circumference is about 11 inches. On the other part of the hole many geometrical designs are made to make it more beautiful and attractive. This is called *'Yongmen'* in Ao dialect. When the girl grows upto 14 to 16 years old, one end of the coiled rod is pressed in the upper hole of the ear lobe and it is turned slowly and slowly till the whole ring is put in the ear holes. The same process is followed in the other side of the ear. Now, these two big brass rings are tied together with a bunch of black threads and put over the head after combing the hair properly with the help of a bamboo splinter comb.

The use of the this ear-ring signifies that the girl has attained marriageable age and is capable of bearing children. By wearing this, ornament on the head, there is no chance for the hair to fall even during the windy season. It adds to the beauty of the girl. This ear-ring is worn by all Ao women folk irrespective of rich and poor, high and low. The Ao women wears this for all occasions, both festival and casual. In the district of Phek, the Chakhesang women use this ear-ring like that of the Ao women but they are little bigger in size and one round only. It is made up of brass wire and they call it *Mesunyi*. In the district of Kohima, the Zeliang women folk wear this kind of ear-ring having similarity to that of the Aos and the Chakhesangs. The making process of such ear-ring is little different from one tribe to another tribe. The two ends of the Naga ear-ring are little bigger just like funnel shape, but the middle portion is small and narrow and coiled twice. Right and left ear-rings are tied with a small bunch of thread and put over the head like earphone type connecting both the ear-ring properly. It is made up of brass rod. This is known as *Enhengoi-e* in Zeliang dialect.

In the district of Zunheboto, the women folk of the Sema tribe wear a typical kind of such ornament to keep their hair intact and elegant. For making such ornament, a splint of bamboo is thinned out and the two ends are bound together to make it round in shape. On the outer part, the bamboo plaited designs are made with red cane fibres and yellow orchids skin. Many typical designs of flowers are knitted with red cane and yellow orchid skin to make it more beautiful and attractive. This ornament is known as *Aghu-u* in Sema dialect.

Also, in the district of Tuensang, the Phom women folk wear a small hair band. It is very much similar to that of the Sema hair band. For making this ornament, red cane fibre and yellow orchid skin are required. This is known as *Kovok* in Phom dialect.

2.2 The Hair Band

Hair is one of the most beautiful qualities of a woman. Therefore, the personality of a woman is also judged by the quality of the hair she possesses. Falling of hair or greying naturally takes place less among the female members. Except minor girls, women don't shave their hair because it is considered to be one of the physical qualities of a woman. Man perhaps would not admire a woman who is not gifted with hair. Naturally, a woman may attract a man by her attractive hair, which is the pride of a woman.

Hair is a non-elastic, smooth and silky fibre, and has no blood. When it is not maintained properly, it looks untidy. Traditionally, most of the Naga women folk have either bun or braid hair but hairstyle has undergone many changes. Since hair is non-elastic, smooth and silky, there is tendency of loosing the hair bun easily. Therefore, the Naga women use a variety of hair bands to tie round the bun to stop the loosing of hairs. Apart from binding the bun the hair band also adds beauty and colour to the women folk.

Among the women folk of the Ao tribe there are two fashions for binding the buns i.e. *Mongsen* and *Jungli* fashions. Story tells us that among the Aos, the *Mongsen* phraty first invented the use of yarn and so the *Mongsen* women folk bind the bun round with string made of white thread. In *Mongsen* dialect, the white string which bind the bun is called *Lemlangvi.* On the other hand the *Jungli* phraty use hair band made of fallen hair that had been collected which looks silky and shining. This hair band is known as *Kopok.* Both *Lemlangvi* and *Kopok* are used during festival and casual occasions.

The Lotha women in the district of Wokha also bun their hair. They collect the fallen hairs and make their band. This is called *Tsantsu.* They use it throughout their life which beautifies them. In Zunheboto district, the Sema women folk also bind their hair band which is also made of fallen hair. This is called *Asakipili.* This *asakipili* makes the bun beautiful and grand looking. They use new one during the festival time and the older one in normal occasion. In the district of Phek, the Chakhesang women also make their band collecting the fallen hair from the very beginning. This is known as *Pizhie* and sometimes they also use white thread to make their band. The use of these hair bands glorifies the Chakhesang women folk.

In Kohima district, use of traditional hair band among the Angamis, the Rengmas and the Zeliangs is very common. They also use hair band by collecting the fallen hairs. This is thicker and longer artificially. They also braid their hair which is known as *Tsuchuro* and *Tsusurie.* The hair round the bun makes the Angami women folk more beautiful, attractive and dignified. The Rengma women also collect the fallen hairs and make hair band which is known as *Alasapvu.* The Zeliang women also adopt the similar method of hair band which is called *Poitua.* It adds colour to the beauty of the Zeliang women.

In Mon district, the Konyak women use strings of thread besides a variety of leaves for making hair band. They call it *Shangwi* and hair band is called *Sangtum.*

In Tuensang district, tribes like Phom, the Sangtams, the Changs, the Yimchungers and the Khiamngians also bun their hair. The women folk of the Phom collect their fallen hairs and use them for making hair band. This is called *Shoshanpakvi* or *Kongedyie* with which the buns are bound. The hair bun is called *Shoshadam.* The Sangtam women also use thread and fallen hairs as hair band. They call it *Kumakhi* which is used on all occasions. The Chang women use both the fallen hairs and the thread to make hair band to tie round the bun. This is known as *Kotep* which is used for all times. The Yimchunger women also collect the fallen hairs for making hair band. Sometimes threads are used for the purpose. The Khiamungian women use the fallen hairs for making their hair band. This is known as *Khainke.* The use of such variety or ornamental items by Naga women folk makes the Naga culture richer and more beautiful

2.3 The Crystal Earring

God has reserved precious wealth for mankind in the depth of the sea in the interior of the earth, and wisdom to explore and extract these precious deposits to meet their needs. Man intelligently searched and extracted those precious wealth like gold, silver, precious stones, iron etc. from the depth of the earth and the sea. Among them, is the crystal marble, which is hard clear shining mineral used for making of special ear-ring. Cutting and polishing of this crystal marble is a delicate and difficult task which can be done only by the expert craftsman. These materials are then used for making ornaments. The ear-ring made of such crystal marble is a very costly ornament. A pair of such ear-rings cost Rs. 90 to 100 during the early 19th century.

In those days 16 annas, made one rupee. A days wage of a man was only one anna which means sixteen persons were engaged to earn one rupee a day. After the end of the Second World War, a day's wage became 2 annas. Though the value of money was very high in those days, people used to buy such costly ornaments with high prices.

There are two types of ear-ring use by Naga women folk. One is round and the other is square in shape. An ear-ring measures about two inches long by one and half inches breadth, and is about half inch in thickness. There is a round hole in the middle of the ear-ring joint to the edge by a slit to admit the hole of the ear which is pierced for this purpose; and it is worn with the slit downward. The origin of this ornament and how it came to our land remains obscure. During those days, the Naga women preferred to wear this ornament and they were so ambitious to collect such costly ornaments from different countries.

The use of gold by the Nagas in the past is not fully known. In the absence of gold, crystal ornament was regarded as one of the highest valued wealth among the Nagas. In Nagaland, there are some tribes who mostly wear the crystal ear-ring. Among them are the Aos, the Sangtams, the Yimchungers, the Phoms etc. It is not a festival ornament but the Naga women use to wear it in all times. Even while sleeping they wore such heavy ornaments. Once it is put in the lower holes of the ears, it was removed only when one dies was the normal practice. This crystal ear-ring is known as *Tongpang* in Ao dialect. They believed that crystal ear-rings have magical charming power. There are interesting stories, depicting how the womenfolk wore such ornament with their faces shining at night and charmed their male counterparts.

The women folk of Mon district, wear similar ear-rings. They use both round and square type of ear-rings. They call it *Naju*. Since this is a costly ornament, it is popularly worn by the *Ahngs*' wives, though it is used by other women folk too.

In Tuensang district, the women folk of Phom tribe also use similar ear-rings as used by the Aos and the Konyaks. This is called *Chushok*. The Sangtam tribe also use both the types of ear-rings; but the round one is more popular among them. This is known as *Naugvi*. The Khiamngan women also wear both the types; but the round one is more popular among them. They call this as *Nataú*. Among the Yimchunger women folk both the round and square shapes are commonly used; but the round type is more popular. They call this ear-ring as *Thsungkhiuki*. The Chang women also wear both types, but they prefer the round shape most. Thus, the use of various types of ear-rings among the Naga women folk are found to be so common.

The crystal ear-ring is generally a women's dress in Naga society. However,the manfolk also put ear-ring which is round in shape. This is very popular among the older persons. The wearing of such ear-ring among the male members is now disappearing slowly. During dancing they put flowers, cotton, weeds, leaf etc. in their ear holes.

It is interesting to note that the Burmese word *Naka* is the origin of the word, Naga. In Burmese, *Na* means, ear; *Ka* means, pierced i.e. the one who pierced his ear and therefore named as *Naka*. In fact, Naga men and women to pierce their ears and they put flowers and creepers as they are lovers of natural beauty. In the past, a person whose ears are not pierced was not regarded as a real Naga. That is why we clearly notice every Naga by tradition having ear holes especially those who were born before fifties. Today, one will find many elderly persons wearing the original ear-ring in the villages, because, it is their culture and tradition brought from the original place of their migration.

2 . The Necklace

There are many interesting stories related to various items of Naga traditional dresses. For instance, the use and origin of necklace *Azuk* has its own story. This is made of semi-precious stones of a reddish colour found to be very popular among all tribes of Naga women. They have been using this right from the time of early civilization.

Story tells us that once upon a time, there was a village called Mongyim in which lived a beautiful girl called Pathu. Her parents were extremely poor and could not afford to give her anything more than two meals a day. Pathu felt very unhappy. She could not tolerate the sufferings for which she wept bitterly every day. Many a time, she asked herself in wonder as to why such misery came to her family and how to overcome it. But she did not show her pain to her parents; and she always struggled with a smiling face even before her friends. She was very intelligent and honest but had no false pride. Since she was an expert girl in all other household matters, she was admired by many rich and handsome youngmen and many were interested to marry her. Her parents too wished her to get married to a rich man's son but she did not agree with her parents wish. She said to her parents, "if I marry a rich man, sometimes when un-favourable conditions occur at home, they may not know the sad aspects of human life. So for me, it is better not to get married. It is better to avoid them". It was at this time, when she was still indecisive, that a handsome young man from a poor family, proposed to marry her. She readily agreed and they were happily united in marriage. They both laboured hard with dignity and had no time to quarrel at home. They favoured high dignity of hard working and honesty. Just when the summer began, they got a baby son. The parents were filled with joy and happiness. The father was so excited that he sang a song of praise and happiness.

"The sun has risen, a new day has begun,
God of Creator to be praised,
For his blessing added unto us,
Let my son and mother be protected,
When the warrior fought away from home"

(English Translation)

When the child attained six months old he displayed his short temper before his mother while feeding him on her breast. At times, when the baby start crying the mother always tried to soften him in a low voice of the same song of praise and happiness sung by her husband. But it was very difficult for her to control her baby. She was always thinking as to how to discover some methods to control the child's temper. One day, the mother played a trick just to control the movements of her child while crying. She tied a big cotton thread on her neck. When the baby woke up from deep slumber, the mother took him in her arms as usual. When he started cyring, she held her hand on the thread so as to stop him from crying and fed her breast milk. After that, there was no problem for feeding the child who always played merrily with the thread string and he never cried. The same method was repeated while feeding the child. Other mother's also copied this device putting some beads on them. Those who were rich used to put some other ornamental stones also. Later on, all women applied this method and in this way the use of beads necklace came into being. In Ao, this is called *Azuk* which means the child holding hand, *Azuk* thus, became popular among all women folk.

The use of Cornelian beads necklace became more popular since 18th century. More attraction and demand was added when Mr. Tsüktimeren of Akhoia happened to reach Kongthu (Now Jorhat long ago.) He was a pioneering trader. He saw Cornelian beads for the first time in Jorhat which attracted him most. he thought that such item could be loved by the Aos to be worn during festival of the Aos and other special occasions especially by the rich persons during *mithun* celebration feast. He discussed this matter secretly with one of his very closed friends name, Jishitongpang from the same village. These two friends from Akhoia village went to Jorhat and bought some beads for making necklace including some other items of ornaments loved by the Aos and other Naga tribes. They brought them to Molung village and sold them there at one stroke. Thus, the first load was sold out to be Molung villagers alone. They went to Jorhat again and brought the same ornament and sold out to the next villagers, Molungyimsen. The third load of necklace made of Cornelian beads was then sold at Imchenkimong village. They did not go back to their village till they sold out several loads of beads in Changkikong range. In their next mission they went to Kangtsung, Wameken, Anaki and Merangkong villages in lower portion of Langpangkong range in Mokokchung district of Nagaland. At last, they returned back to their own village, Akhoia with huge amount of money at that time. In this way, Jishitongpang and Tsüktimeren became very popular; and they became very rich persons in the region. They were the wholesalers and the main agents of various ornaments, salt, iron and other precious items. Thus, the use of necklace became more popular and became a common dress of Naga women.

The women all over the world like to put on something on their neck which is called necklace. The Nagas are no exception and they too designed their own necklace from clay, stone, brass and silver. Moreover, they used conch shell which is found in the deep sea. Many varieties of ornaments are made out of those shells both for men and women. The Angami women use colourful oval shaped Cornelian beads, made out of shells having ten rows even. This is used on special days or occasion like Sakrenyie festival. It is worn by the womenfolk and attracts the spectators with great joy and happiness. They called this necklace *Tsudzie*. This is not only a festival necklace but can be used on any occasion. A similar necklace is also worn by the Chakhesang women. They wear it specially on national festival like *Sakhranyie* days. They call them *Teiza*. Among the Zeliang community, the womenfolk wear this necklace during *Ngu-ngai* festival dance. The Zeliang people perform different dances wearing this particular necklace. They call it *Teuba*. The same made of precious stone is also worn by the Rengma womenfolk. This is one of the most popular necklace among the Rengmas. They wear it during their *Ngada* festival dance which make them more grand looking and beautiful. They call this necklace *Tephuthong*. Similar ornaments are used by the Lotha women known as *Tsuro* which is also very beautiful and attractive. They wear it during *Tokho Emong* festival day. The people of Zunheboto district of Sema community specially the womenfolk wear this necklace made of precious stones during their *Tuluni* festival dance. it fits them more beautifully on every occasion, They call it *Achigho*.

The womenfolk of Ao community wear a variety of beads necklace like Wangkum, Poklang, Sangshi etc. arranged in a bunch. Such necklaces are used not only during festival but in normal times also. Among the above mentioned beads, Sangshi is more precious which is made up of pure brass and silver, There are two national festivals of the Aos, *Moatsu* and *Tsungrem-Mong*. On these particular occasions the women folk wear colourful ornaments and perform dances. the Sangshi necklace glitters just like the reflection of the sun's rays on the high altitude of snow falling mountains. They call this necklace as *Sangshizuk*. The other tribes in Tuensang district like the Sangtams, the Yimchungers, the Phoms, the Khiamngians, and the Changs also have different kinds of necklaces. The Sangtam women wear *Sanghsi* similar to that of the necklace worn by the Ao girls. They wear Sanghsi along with other varieties of colourful beads during *Amongmong* festival

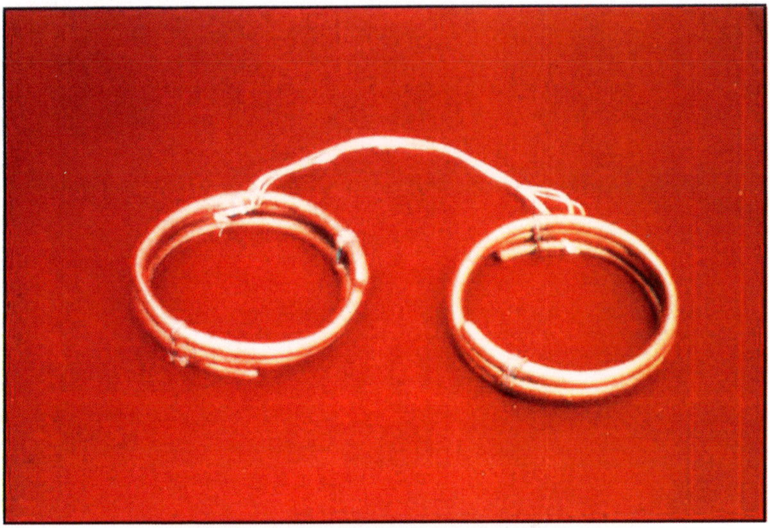

Fig. 2.1 : The Brass Hair Band

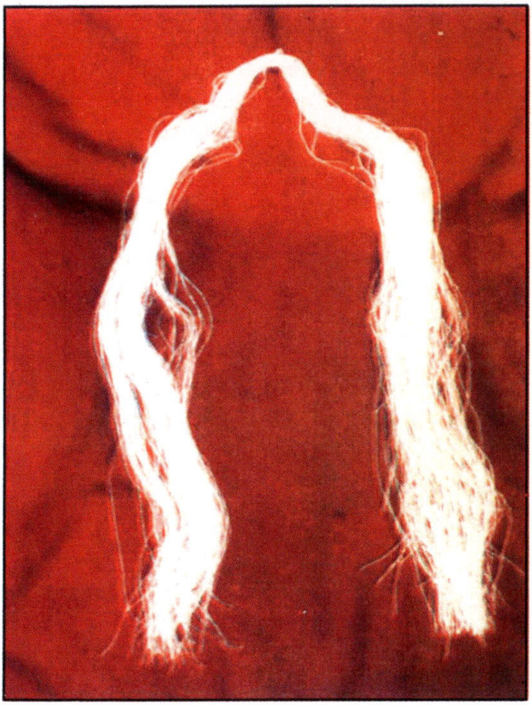

Fig. 2.2 : The Hair Band

Fig. 2.3 : The Crystal Earring

Fig. 2.4A : The Necklace

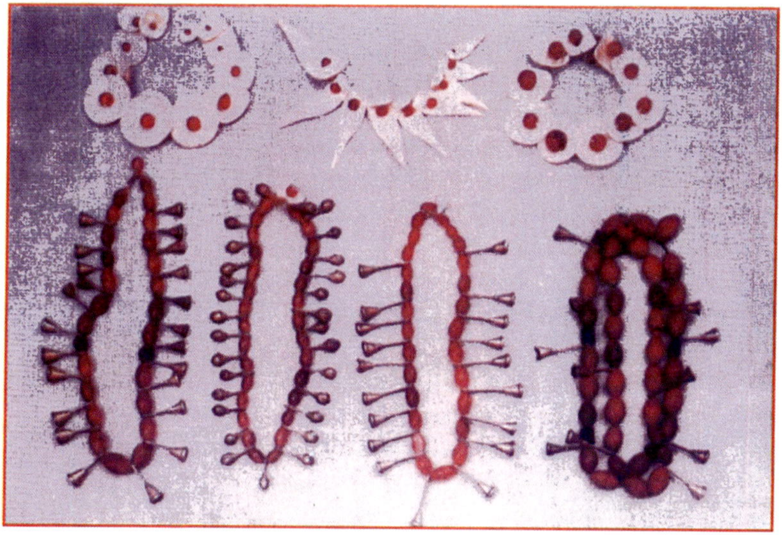

Fig. 2.4B : The Necklace

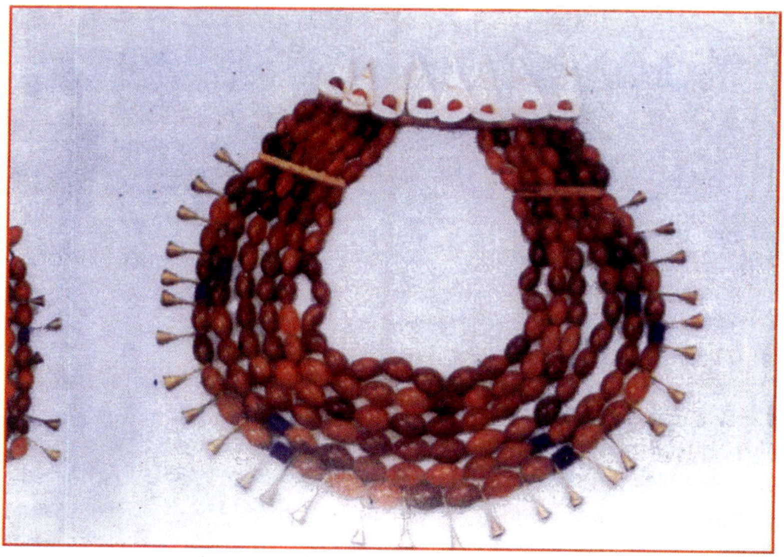

Fig. 2.4C : The Necklace

dances. This necklace is known a *Lak* in Sangtam dialect. The Yimchunger women use Sangshi mixed with other kinds of beads. The necklace worn by them is called *Sunsolak* which they wear mainly during the merry making festival of national importance. The women of Phom also have similar Cornelian bead necklaces but slightly different in size and colour as used by other tribes. They use it both during festival and normal times. The Khiamngian girls use similar ornaments which are much smaller but more valuable in comparison to other necklace of the other Naga tribes as mentioned above. This is the best traditional necklace of Khiamngian tribe of Tuensang district. Women wear this necklace while dancing in the festivals of *Miu* and *Tzukom*. The Chang girls also use valuable ornaments similar to that of the other tribes. They use all colours mixed with other variety of beads. It is an attractively arranged necklace with many different beads called *Yak*. They use this necklace during their national days like *Nknyulum*. The women and girls of Konyak Nagas too have many kinds of bead necklaces quite different from other Naga tribes. Each piece is very small in size and so it is very difficult to arrange into a bunch necklace. They are of many different colours. They have their own techniques of arrangement without any trouble and hardship. This necklace looks like a rainbow shining on the chest of a beautiful girl. They wear these ornaments during *Aoling Mong* festival. Likewise, different Naga tribes use different kinds of Cornelian beads exhibiting the rich Naga culture.

2.5 The Women Bodice

Everyone is born naked and every individual gets dressed as per the needs of the time and environment. In the past, the Nagas were called the naked by many foreigners because the Nagas did not wear enough dress due to paucity of cloths. The fashion and style of dressing was so simple exhibiting the natural beauty of a person. Even the womenfolk did not wear petticoat nor brassiere during the olden days. However, due to the influence of modern civilization the Nagas had picked up modern fashion within a short span of time.

In the past, the use of the bodice by women (popularly known as brassiere) was not at all known in Naga society. In place of modern brassiere, the Naga women wore bodice which was just a piece of shawl used in order to cover the chest. Different Naga tribes wore different types of bodice as their fashion in traditional way.

In olden days, the women of different tribes used only a piece of shawl to cover the upper part of their chest covering the breasts. Some tribal women did not wear anything even to cover their breasts. Breasts were exposed openly without any feeling because it was their way of life.

The women of Sema, Lotha, and some other tribes in the central part of Nagaland used two different shawls for different purposes namely, normal and jungle purpose. When they worked in the jungles, they used a particular shawl for that purpose. In this way, they tied two corners of one end of the shawl under one armpit and put a simple double knot over the shoulder of the other arm and folded the shawl on their back to put a similar knot over the other arm. In this way, the breasts was covered partly. The Ao women also used the shawl in the similar way while working in the jungle or in the field. In addition to this, they used bodice exclusively for the purpose of covering their breasts. The women folk of the Angamis, the Chakhesangs and the Tangkhuls also used a specially designed cloth to cover their breasts.

The bodice *(Tukutsukresü* in Ao dialect) used by the Ao girl is regarded as a holy dress because it is made in a holy way. The girls use this bodice for the first time just after the date of maturity, when they feel uneasy due to sudden onset of menstruation period; they report to their mother that they cannot attend their daily work due to health problem. Health problem without any specified disease at that particular age gives an indication to the mother that she has reached maturity. Just after this information is given, the mother starts the process of weaving a bodice for her daughter. The mother also maintains purity at least for 6 days by informing her husband to avoid sex during this period. After the purity period is over, she starts weaving the bodice. This is a simple piece of cloth made of either white or black or blue thread. The size of the cloth depends on the chest of the user. Normally, it is around 4 to 5 feet and 1 foot wide. Now-a-days, when the young girls are dressing themselves for the purposes of a festival dance, they use the same bodice in two different width. Some use shorter width (as it was in traditional days) just enough to cover the breasts nicely and it does not touch the skirt. But some others use much wider (almost double in width of the traditional ones) bodice to touch or slightly covering their skirts. This bodice is just wrapped round their chest tightly to cover their breasts. A corner of the outer end of the force is pushed while wrapping so that it does not fall down. After a week or ten days of their maturity, the girls of the Ao tribe were socially bound to wear bodice, even if they use a shawl to cover their body. They were bound to use bodice till they were married and blessed with a child. When a woman becomes a mother it depends on her personal choice and comfort to use a bodice or not.

As used in some parts of eastern India, the use of a blouse in a lower and lower middle class society is normally associated with the age of a woman. The use of bodice has nothing to do with the age or socio-economic status. If a girl remains unmarried or a married woman remains without issue she is socially bound to use bodice for the whole life. While a young mother can move freely exposing her breasts, an unmarried or childless old lady is bound to use the bodice on her shrinken chest, of course, after a certain age i.e. 55 to 60 years; violation to this social practice is not taken seriously and people do not view at all even a very old unmarried or childless woman who do not use bodice. Even the childless widows use bodice during their young age. After death, when the dead body of a woman (unmarried matured girl or issueless woman) is taken to the funeral ground it is decorated with all her cloths including this bodice. According to Ao custom, no one is allowed to touch this cloth because it is against their social norms.

This bodice is regarded as having the following functions:

1. To cover the sex appealing private parts particularly from male members of the society.
2. To provide comfort particularly at the time of field work, household work and speedy walk on the village street. It prevents the bouncing of the breasts due to wrapping tightly.
3. To add to the beauty of a young woman because it is horizontal wrapping over the chest between their skirt and hairy head with a decorated neck. The muscular strip under the fair and charming skin looks attractive between the bodice and skirt.
4. To work as a background plate for the ornaments use on their neck particularly the luckers (called Sangshi in Ao dialect) of the necklace.
5. To serve as a towel for soaking sweat excreated by the skin during long hard working hours in the field. More often they use one corner as a towel on their sweaty face.

In the southern part of the State of Nagaland, women of three tribes are reported to have had different types of bodice to protect the private part over their chest. An ordinary Angami lady wear *Neikhro* (petticoat) and *Vatchu* (bodice). Vatchu crosses under the left arm and fastens on the opposite shoulder and the lower end touches the knee up to *Neikhro. Vatchu* is usually made of black thread. The Angami girl child is taught and trained to weave small cloths at an early age to begin with; and subsequently, larger and wearable sizes when she grows up. They start using their *Vatchu* during their adolescence stage even before their maturity. Some girls though ordinarily may not wear Vatchu every day; are asked to wear it on some important festival days. There is no such restriction in making *Vatchu* as it is with the Ao tribe where the mother can do so only after maintaining purity to make a bodice to be used for the first time by her daughter after maturity. The Tangkhul ladies use a bodice called *Sihup* in Tangkhul which is wrapped round the breasts just below the arm pit touching the skirt at the waist just like a long bodice used by Ao girls. The Chakhesang girls also wear their own bodice called *Sükhüthoü.* They wear two rectangular piece of cloths of equal size. The body of this cloth is black, or blue with a red border of around one inch width. Both the ends of this cloth have a thin yellow line. The first piece of cloth is usually taken under the left arm in such a way that both the upper corner meet the opposite shoulder for fastening of a knot. Similarly, the other piece or cloth is taken under the right arm. When a knot is put on the left shoulder with the help of both the upper ends corners, both the end of the cloth fall opening longitudinally over the body in the left hand side because there is no knot with the lower end corners. The lower border of both the cloths overlap the skirt on waist. Since the cloths are taken under the arm, the hands are not disturbed for the movement. In the middle and northern part of the State of Nagaland, women of many tribes did not have any well established dress to cover their breasts. They used a single piece of cloth wrapped under the arms to cover the body up to their knees.

This is a simple and general presentation about the bodice of the Naga women used in traditional society. Moreover, one will find a sifnificant change in the traditional dresses of the Nagas which is taking place so fast now-a-days. The Naga boys and girls have already adopted western culture, and the living style of life has totally been westernised today.

2.6 The Mekhala

Different people of different countries wear different fashions on different occasions. They have their styles of manufacturing and wearing different dresses and apparels according to their choice, liking, tradition and customs. Such dresses and apparels suit different races of the world in their own likeness.

In this article an attempt has been made to explain different types of mekhala or skirt worn by Naga women. One can claim that in reality, the garment worn by Naga women is not actually a skirt because the skirt in its own fashion was not known to the Nagas in the past. Rather, it is more appropriate to call it as the waist wrapper; because the apparel used by the Naga women wrap the whole hip and legs reaching just above the ankles. It is not a real skirt as worn by other non-Naga women. It is a traditional Naga women's dress in the their own style having different local names, styles, designs and colours which are very attractive. In Ao dialect it is called *Süpeti* or Teperemsü (*teperem* means the waist, *sü* means the cloth) i.e. the cloth or garment put on the waist, wrapping the whole hip from right to left direction covering the legs in the form of a skirt, commonly called *Mekhala*; the waist wrapper, *Süpeti*.

Nagaland is inhabited by many colourful tribes. The Naga women are gifted with more creative talents. Women are expert weavers and thus they produce sufficient cloths with variety of colourful designs. They wear different traditional garments which are very attractive. These traditional dresses looks very grand and so colourful. Hence it makes the Naga culture rich, and attractive. Every tribe wear different types of *mekhala* and within one tribe also, different clans wear different types of such *mekhala* indicating different significant meanings. Each tribal traditional *mekhala* are so distincitve and so is the case of different clans.

The Ao women wear various types of *Supeti* like '*Angnensü*', *Angnaksü* and *süpasü* etc. as in case of other tribes. They wear such traditional dresses with great enthusiasm specially during festivals. The *mera süpeti* is a special type of apparel which is worn during special occasions.

The Chakhesang women too wear many types of *mekhalas*. *Muyhone* is one of the most beautiful one liked by them. It is little similar to *Tangkutepsü* (i.e. the Mongsen dialect of the Ao Naga tribe) of the Aos with a decorated middle band or stripe. The middle band is small in size and is transfixed between the two wider segments like Tangkutepsü. The looms of two wider segments are made with yarns of white and orange colour and woven with black colour fibre. The middle band is designed by white yarn and woven with yellow and green yarns with colourful curving designs. There is no lace on both ends of the *mekhala*. This is generally worn with a blouse called *Suhk Wuthsu*, which looks very beautiful. During festival *Tsukhenyi* day, the on lookers are charmed and hypnotised by the beautiful dress of the young dancers.

Surhum is the most beautiful and popular *mekhala* of the Lotha women. This is similar to that of the Chakhesang women in many ways with a small middle band between two wider segments. The loom of the two wider pieces are made with green at the outer border and four stripes of green, orange, red and black. The loom prepared is woven with black yarn. The lower segment will again be laced with attractive decoration of different colours and designs of her liking. The loom of the middle band is made up of blue, red, orange and black and woven by skyblue yarn. Here also the weaver can put curving designs here and there in colour of her choice. This particular *mekhala* is worn compulsorily by the Lotha womenfolk during *Tokhu Emong*, the most important festival of the Lotha Nagas.

The Khimnngans are fair and handsome people. Their womenfolk also wear various types of *mekhala* and the most popular one is called *Necham*. The loom of this *mekhala* is made with black yarn and woven again in black with a white horizontal stripes somewhere in the beginning. Black colour is very popular among them. The *mekhala* has no lace and it is worn during *Miu* and *Tsoküm* festivals.

The mekhala of the Chang Nagas also differs from clan to clan. The most popular amongst them is called *Sosobü*. The loom of this *mekhala* is made with a number of colours starting from black followed by a stripes of black, red and blue and again followed by four wide bands of red. In between the red bands, there are three smaller bands in blue. The loom so made will now be woven in sheer red complete with lace on both sides of the end. A number of colourful designs are put in the black while in the blue bands a particular rhombus design is woven in red. Both the segments of the *mekhala* are made in the same way and joined together with black bands of both the segments coming together in the middle.

Mongsum Ashak is the most important of all the *mekhalas* worn by Phom women. It is made up of two similar segments. The loom is made in black, red and white and woven in red throughout. The middle white band is dotted with a host of curving designs. There is no lace on the borders.

Similarly, the Sangtam ladies wear a number of colourful *mekhalas* but the most pupular one is called *Shuringthsi Puküm*. The loom of this wrapper is made with alternate mixture of yellow, green, red and black. The black band is wider and more prominent throughout. Inside the yellow, green and red bands a spurt of creative designs are woven with red yarns. The two segments are made similarly and stitched together. There are short laces on both sides of the borders.

The Angami ladies are also very expert in making and designing their colourful waist wrappers. The most popular one is called *Pfhemhou*. This *mekhala* is also made up of two segments woven similarly. The loom is made prominent in white with smaller bands of green, red and black here and there and woven in sheer white. In the white band, a number of designs are put in red and black colours. There is no lace on either side. The two segments so made are then stitched together with white, meeting together in the middle. The women wear such *mekhala* so stylishly with the hem of one side sliding down slightly more than the other one and it looks so charming on them. They wear this wrapper in all their manifold festivals and important occasion too.

The *mekhala* of the Rengma women are similar to that of the Chakhesang counterparts in many ways. Their most popular *mekhala* is called *Mimenyu*. It is made up of two segments with a white band at the middle. The loom of this *mekhala* is made with white yarn. The small white band is mde separately and sandwiched between two principal segments.

The most popular *mekhala* of the Zeliang women is *Gikli*. It is also composed of two segments made in the same way. The loom of the wrappers is made in red, black and white and woven completely in black. In the white band, lot of designs are put in a variety of colours and the end of the threads are left hanging at the border. The two segments are now stitched together to make the skirt complete. The Zeliang women wear it covering the breasts leaving the upper chest bare.

There are quite a good number of traditional *mekhalas* worn by Sema women. The most popular of them all is *Tsunghumi*. This is also composed of two small parts. The loom of the first part is made up of red, yellow and black upto the middle followed by two rows of blue. Every row will again be transferred with green, black, yellow, red and skyblue. The loom is woven in black. The second part is also made similarly but the curving design is put only on one side. The two segments are stitched together to complete the *mekhala*. There is another garment worn over the wrapper called *Akicholachi*. It is made up of different colours of beads like blue, brown and yellow and stitched them together to fit the waist of the wearer. The garment is worn by pulling over the *mekhala*.

The most popular *mekhala* of the Konyak women is called *Nyiha*. It is also made up of two segments. The loom of the first part is made with four white bands and three bands of red and black mixed together followed by another band of red and black towards the end. This is bounded by two bands of red and black on either side with a number of creative designs in red and black. In the mixed band a curving of red and black design similar to that of the Chakhesang is put with red and black yarns. The second part is also made similarly and is woven in white throughout with provision for making lace on the border. The two segments are then stitched together with the white bands coming together in the middle. This is the most prestigious and popular *mekhala* of the Konyak women. They wear it on all important festivals and occasions.

Thus the Naga women wear different types of *mekhalas* woven by themselves with decorated designs. Each tribe wears different *mekhala* indicating their tribes. Even within the same tribe, each clan use to wear different types of *mekhala* indicating their clan's affiliation in their community. It makes a colourful community with rich cultural heritage.

In the past, Naga women never wore Salwar-Kamez, skirt, longi, or sari. But now-a-days, use of salwar dresses have become popular mainly for two reasons. Firstly, economically it is much cheaper than the woven *mekhala* and shawls and, secondly they are more comfortable and convenient on all occasions. However, wearing of *sari* is still not so common among the Naga women. But wearing of Jean Pants have become very common amongst the youngsters. Wearing of longi is not adopted by the Nagas.

2.7 The Bangle

The bangles worn by woman is one of the most beautiful ornaments all over the world. Normally, men do not wear bangles. By nature, the arms of women are soft and attractive. To add more lustre they wear variety of bangles made of different materials. The bangles produce a pleasant sound too while working and dancing. Its sound is very sweet and enjoyable by everybody. The bangles which are made of gold, silver, tin and copper etc, are more costlier than other ordinary bangles.

Story tells us that in course of Naga migration from the Central and South East Asia; they carried a variety of precious ornaments including the bangles at different period of times. Those ornaments are considered to be the most original ornaments used by the Nagas even today.

The bangles worn by the Naga women are made of brass, metal

and copper. They are rather very heavy and solid. They are not just ordinary bangles. During the early centuries, the brass, the metal and the copper etc. were not available in their region. Yet, they put bangles made of such materials. They do wear coils of shining spirals which stretch their brassneck. Most probably, the parent countries from where they migrated might have supplied shining bangles to the Naga people, even after they left the original place. Thus, the use of bangles became popular among the Nagas since early days.

Among the Aos, there is a blacksmith clan who make bangles. This clan manufacture two types of bangles, i.e. the bangle to be used during festivals only and the other is for casual purpose. The Ao women wear one or two bangles in each wrist as a fashion. They shine it with the juice of sour fruits and ordinary ashes. Festival bangles are made in a special way. The size of the metal should be as big as a thumb at both ends. In the middle of the curve, some curving like fins of fish is printed. In case of casual wear, the size of the metal is then which can be conveniently worn for all occasions. These are very matching ornaments to women because it gives a grand appearance during the festivals of *Moatsu* and *Tsungrem Mong*. They called it *''Kisen''*.

Bangles are popularly worn by the Lotha women too. Both young and old wear it as a common fashion. The bangles are inherited by the next kin in case of natural death. In case of unnatural death *(Aputia)* not only bangle but all articles belonging to the deceased are not used unless they are purified by the village priest. There is a common understanding among the parents that they should procure enough bangles for their children. Young lads can wear bangles but they have to give up when they reach adolescent age. These bangles are known as *Rembum* in Lotha.

The Sema women also love to wear bangles. Both young and old women wear it on all occasions. Before adolescent stage, even young lads can wear it. Among the Nagas, the Sema women are more fond of wearing the maximum number of bangles from wrist to elbow. The chief's wife wear the bend coils of a single piece of metal from wrist to the elbow. This peculiar type of coil of a single piece of metal bangle suited very well for a Sema woman. They call it *Asapu*.

Bangle is a popular ornament among the Chakhesang women for both young and old. They also use two types of bangles. The first one is a thin and shinning one. Three or four pieces of such bangles can be worn in the wrist. The second type is a flat one and both ends are of trumpet like shape. This is worn in the middle of both the arms. Men of Angami, Chakhesang, and Zeliang wear aprons which cover the

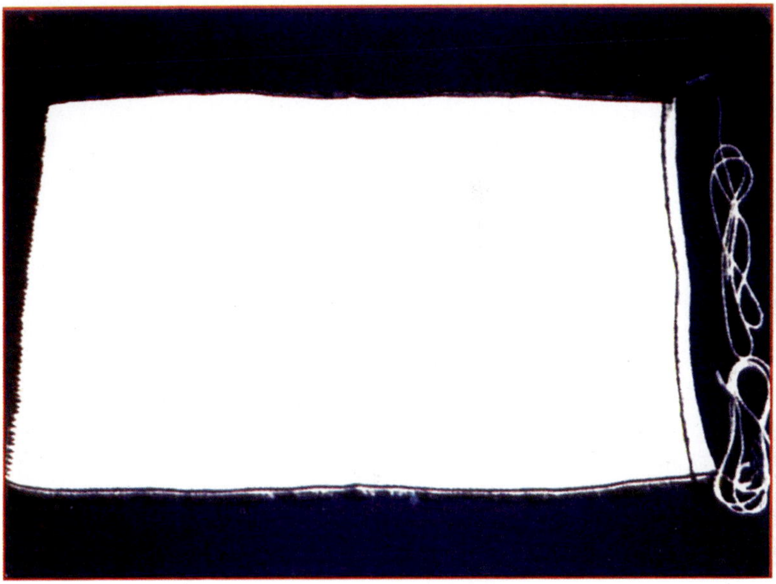

Fig. 2.5 : The Women Bodice

Fig. 2.6 : The Mekhala

Fig. 2.7 : The Bangle

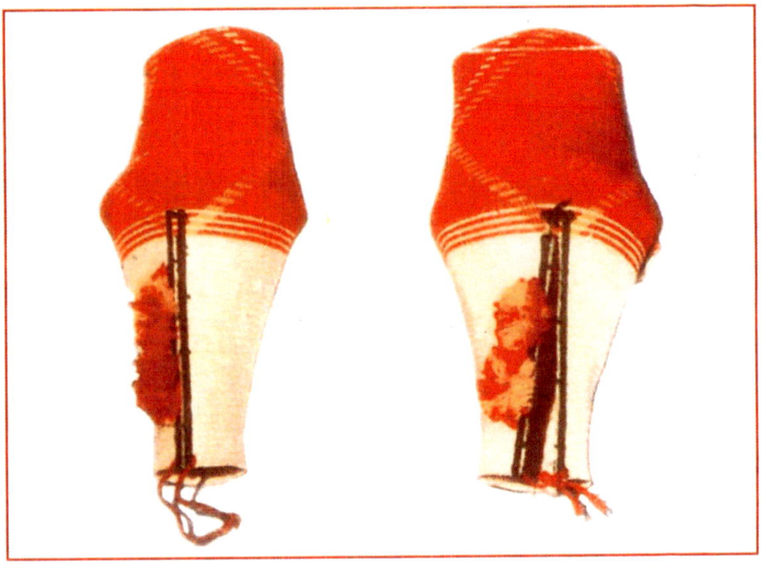

Fig. 2.8 : The Puttees

whole buttock, so also women of these tribes wear the second type of bangles. They wear it during important festivals of *Tsukhenyi*. The bangle is known as *Nogu* in Chakhesang.

The Konyaks are very famous in the art or balcksmith. Apart from manufacturing various ornamental items, they are so expert in manufacturing guns. They manufacture beautiful bangles too. Bangle is a popular ornament among the women of Konyak like other tribes. They wear bangles of different designs and colours. They are mostly made of brass and is constantly polished with juice of sour fruits. They wear them during the *Aoling Mong* festival. Bangle is known as Shuptet in Konyak.

The women of Angamis are also fond of wearing bangles. Even today most of the village women wear it. They use special type of bangles during festivals like *Sekrenyie*. Both ends of the bangles are thicker than the middle curve which gives rare attraction to it. It is called *Thoukie* in Angami. It is regarded as the women's armlet in their culture. It fits them nicely on any occasion.

The Zeliangs are also fond of bangles specially during dancing. They also wear different types of bangles. The casual wear is thin and small but other type is thicker similar to that of the Angami and Chakhesang as mentioned above. This can be used during the festival of *Nga-Ngai* which is observed during the month of December. They call it *Nkitapet.*

The Rengma bangles are of two types. The common bangle is worn from childhood to death. The other type is bigger in size and more decorative than the other one. It is worn only during festival. Like all other tribes of the Nagas they observe their festival in the month of November. On that day, they wear the bangles and dance very elegantly. They call it *Akhwesa*.

The Phom tribe of Tuensang district are also very fond of bangles. They make two types of bangles. One is for casual wear and the other one is for festival occasions only. During *Monyu* festival they wear it and go for dance. This festival is observed during the month of April. They call it *Laktut Nyam* or *Lakap*. Most of the people of Tuensang district are expert in blacksmithy. The Changs can make variety of articles out of metals. Their women are very fond of social life and festive. They wear beautiful bangles during all occasions. They call it *Jikap*. During Naknyulum festival, one can see women wearing bright bangles which are very impressive.

The Yimchunger tribe of Tuensang district are also skilled in blacksmithy. There is a lot of similarities between the Aos and the

Yimchungers. Like the Ao women, the Yimchunger women wear *(Tongpang)* crystal ear-ring and use trumpet shaped necklace *(Sangshi)*. They also love variety of dresses and bangles. Their bangles are made of many coils from a single piece of brass rod. It is worn from wrist up to the elbow. Like the Sema women, they wear it on all occasions. They call it *Aliberukhari*. During their *Metemneo* festival in the month of August, women take active part in dancing wearing beautiful bangles.

The people of Khiamngans live by the side of Myanmar border. They are also expert in blacksmithy and can make many tools and articles out of metal. Bangle is one of the favourite ornament for their women. Two types of bangles are worn by them. One is for casual wear and the other is for festive occasion which is bigger and better. They wear it during their *Miu* and *Tsoküm* festivals. Women take active part during these festivals. They call it *Kiaptso*.

The Sangtams in Tuensang district are also excellent in blacksmithy work. Their women love good dresses and bangles. During *Mongmong* festival they wear it and take active part in dancing which falls in the month of September. Bangle is called *Khehmuyang* or *Bikhum* in Sangtam dialect.

From the above description, it is cleared that the Naga women are fond of wearing two types of bangles, one is for common use whereas the other one is mainly for festival and other special occasions. In the beginning, they brought bangles from neighbouring countries. At present they are making bangles of their own. Use of such ornamental items are found to be so popular among all the tribes of Nagaland as in the case of many other people of different countries.

2.8 The Puttees

The Naga attire consists of many software items. These items are mostly exhibited fully during the occasion of festivals. The Naga *Puttees* is one of them, they wear it during the festival dance. It is worn round the leg from the ankle to the knee for protection and support as a part of their uniforms. Since the legs play an important part in a festival dance, both men and women use it to decorate their legs proportionately. And thereby they gather to the dancing ground with beautiful and attractive dresses. Generally the male dancer use leggings (stockings) whereas the female dancer use *Puttees* to decorate their legs. The *puttees* used by the women is worn in the leg below the knee and above the anklet. This is used commonly by the Ao women.

Shinpong in Ao dialect is considered as an important component while evaluating the overall beauty of a girl. People, particularly the young group use it to watch this part of the leg of their female counterpart when they walk or stand. They evaluate the beauty of the *shin* in terms of several considerations such as colour, shape, length, hairlessness etc. The appearance of a girl is of course considered as the primary factor to judge her beauty, in addition to her facial outlook; several other parts of her body are also considered, of which, shin is one of them. The boys try to evaluate how charming is the colour of the shin of a girl whether it is lengthy shape, hairless, small or muscular and whether it is smooth and soft with tenderness or not etc. A girl having a long, rough and hairy shin is considered as an ugly and given least preference while choosing a life partner. A girl having a hairy shin is considered unlucky and her boys hesitate to extend friendship with her. Similarly, the girls also look at several aspects of boy's physical feature at the time of choosing a boy, either for friendship or life partner. For instance, an Ao girl always looks at the hair cutting of the boy *Kobangtsüng* and evaluates his handsomeness in terms of how nicely he has dressed his hair, how does the hair cutting match his head and how uniformly it is cut and groomed. Since the physical feature is one of the most important considerations in Naga marriage, young boys and girls pay much attention to their physical features and in the process they take care to maintain beauty with all their body parts. There are many instances, that some girls could not marry in time because their shins are disliked by the boys and similarly many boys were unable to get married in time because of their poor hair cutting style etc. The parents, in order to enable their children to get married at the right time always advise them to maintain their beauty of taking care of all parts of their body, especially the shin and *puttee.*

The Naga girls at the time of their festival dance use different kinds of attire decorating themselves more beautifully. They consider festival dance as an occasion to impress their male counterparts. To make their lower legs beautiful, they use *Puttees* called as *Changta* in Ao dialect which is a rectangular piece of white cloth wrapped on their shin, between the anklet and the knee. It looks like wearing stockings. *Puttees* are very simple to wear. It is only an ordinary white cloth rectangular in shape and normally 16 inches in length and 10 inches in width. There is no standard size of a *Puttee;* its length and width depends on the size of the shin of the user. The loom is made of white thread with two thin black lines at both the ends. In a single set-up of the loom, three to four pair of *puttees* are produced. After cutting the long cloth into proper size, both the ends are sealed with circular stitching with the help of a black thread. Two white strings of around 2½ feet in length are tied with the two corners of *the face* end in order to tie the *Puttees* on the shin in such a way that it is conveniently worn and thereby no problem is faced at the time of dancing. The *Puttees* are used to cover the shin in such a way that the border black lines of both the legs remain inward and the people outside (front, back, and sides) cannot see these border lines. The strings are crossed over the skin and both ends of the strings come out from two opposite directions for a final knot inside it.

Though the *Puttees* look very simple, it is not easy to make. Moreover, only selected person can make it as per the custom. The unmarried girls are not allowed to make it, that is to say, only the married women should make it. When the mother feels that her daughter has reached the age to perform dance, she starts making a pair of *Puttees* for her daughter or buys a pair from others. Before setting up the loom for weaving *Puttees,* the Naga women maintain purity atleast for six days. During this purity period, they observe all formalities and keep themselves away from their husbands abstaining from sex. The Nagas are very pious in traditional society. Even if the dress is ready, they do not use it directly unless it is purified. They first sanctiy the *Puttees* by maintaining all formalities and only then they consider that it is ready for use. After use, they wash it and keep in a safe place. So that in the next festival dance they can use it. Once the *Puttees* are sanctified before its first use, it is believed that it is sanctified forever i.e. till its durability.

Another interesting fact associated with this *Puttees* is that, it must first be used once by one of her elder sisters, the elder sister smears indigo leaves on the *Puttees* for two purposes. Firstly, when the leaves are smeared uniformly over the *Puttees* it gives skyblue colour which is more matching for the legs of the women and thereby she goes beautifully with her *mekhala.* Secondly, the smearing of the indigo leaves make the washing of the *Puttees* easier particularly while cleaning the mud marks or dusts from the *Puttees,* which might come at the time of dancing during rainy season festivals.

The *Puttees* can be used both by women and girls at the time of festival dances. But the minor girls are not allowed to use it except during cultural and festival dance.

The use of *Puttees* has several advantages. It protects the shin of a women from injury while working in the forest or on the field. It can maintain smoothness and softness and give psychological satisfaction to her boy friends or life partner. It also protects the legs from cold especially during cold winter. Infact, the old women while sitting at a fire place in order to avoid excess heat to their shins use old *Puttees* for such purpose.

The Ao women are very particular to use such *puttees.* Infact, use of *Puttees* is not popular among other Naga tribes. This is a peculiar dress of the Ao women. All the women irrespective of their status use this dress. There is no distinction between the *Puttees* of a rich woman and a poor woman nor between a married and unmarried woman. The study of this dress has given us a very valuable information that the Ao Nagas had known the use of indigo leaves, since times immemorial for colouring their white dresses. One of the significant reasons of using such item of dress among the Ao women claims that they were more articular to maintain their shins and its exposure during festivals observed during rainy seasons. And during rainy season while dancing the shins are protected from mud and other dirts as the *puttees* keeps her legs properly protected.

2.9 The Women's Shawl

As already mentioned in the preceding paragraphs, the Naga people have different dresses both for man and woman. Since the times immemorial, they used distinct dresses both by man and woman having significant meanings attached to it.

As far as the shawls are concerned, there are different shawls for both man and woman of every Naga tribe. The women are generally prohibited to wear the men's shawl and *vice-versa.* By and large the Naga women folk are very expert in weaving various types of shawl with decorative designs as mentioned above. Free use of indigenous Naga shawl was almost prohibited in the past. But today they are popularising more and more throughout the world. In this unit we shall see various types of the Naga women's shawl of different tribes with different outlook indicating Naga culture and customs.

The Ao women wear varieties of colourful shawls. They use common shawls of different types such as '*Süposü, Sünaksü, angtongsü* etc. Those shawls can be worn on any occasion. The most popular among them is *Angtongsü*. The loom of this shawl is structured with black and blue alternately putting three threads at a time. The loom is now woven with blue colour at the beginning followed by black. The blue and black continues alternately till the end finishing with black. The two segments are then stitched together to make the shawl complete.

There are laces on both sides. There is no damsel who doesn't look beautiful with this shawl.

Again, there are other shawls which are worn exclusively on special occasions and festivals. The most popular among them is *Awosü*. The loom is made alternately in black and blue starting with one inch of black band. In the middle of the loom there is another band of sheer black of about one foot. The loom so made is woven in black. Red wool of about one foot is woven into the shawl on two bands throughout the length of the shawl with one band in the middle and the other near the border. The red wool thus cover the whole of the shawl making it colourful and magnificent with about one foot of red wool hanging all over. There are laces on both sides, another segment will be made in the same way and they are stitched together to complete the shawl. This particular shawl is not commonly worn by other Naga tribes.

Piathi is the most popular shawl of the Zeliang women. The loom of this shawl is made in a mixture of white, black and orange and then followed by another stripe of black and white. This pattern is continued alternatively till the end. The loom so made is then woven by white. Another segment is made similarly. Again, two smaller segments are made by white. All the four segments are then stitched together with the two bigger segments on each side of the border. There are laces only on one side of the shawl.

The Angami women also make and wear a good number of shawls. Their shawl is made up of four small by equal segments. The loom of the two outer segments are made with black, red and green and is woven with black yarn. The two middle segments are loomed and woven in complete black but some designs are woven on one side of the margin. The middle band (stripe) are same for both skirt and shawl of the Angami women. This colourful band identifies an Angami women even from a far off distance.

Anothsü is the most popular shawl of the Rengma women. This shawl is also composed of four segments. The loom of all the segments are made with white yarn dotted here and there with black, green, yellow and woven in white. In the upper-most segment some designs are woven (3 inches) here and there with black, green and yellow. The four segments are now stitched together. A sort of ribbon is made; therefore, laces are not necessary. *Anothsü* is a very beautiful shawl of the Rengma women and it fits them on many occasions.

There are many beautiful shawls of the Lotha women. A shawl called *Opüram* is the most popular of them all. It is made up of two segments made similarly. A great variety of colour is used in making this shawl. The first part of the loom (about one inch) is made alternately in black, green and yellow. This is followed by three wide bands of red sandwiched between three stripes of black, green and yellow. Each stripe is about one inch in width. It is followed by another stripe of black, green and yellow and completed with wide red band at the border. There are four black bands in the shawl and the weaver can put any design she likes on these four black bands. The two borderlines are decorated with curving designs and there are laces on both sides. When the two segments are stitched together, the result will be very colourful making a beautiful shawl.

Kaone is the most important and popular shawl of the Khiamngan women. This shawl may be made in two or three segments, according to the physical structure of the weaver. The loom is made up of black yarn with small ribbon of white here and there and woven in black. There are no laces but the borders are laced with ribbon of white yarn bunding the shawl firmly. One may call it black shawl but spattering of white ribbons make it very attractive.

There are a good number of shawls being made and worn by the Phom women too. Here is an account of '*Phom Lakshong*' one of their most beautiful and popular shawls. This shawl is made up of two big segments similarly made and a small segment in the middle. The loom of the two bigger segments are structured with big bands of red and black alternately. In both black and red bands is dotted with small white stripe. The loom is then woven with black yarn. The smaller middle segment is loomed with four white bands in between small black stripe. In the white bands, the weaver will put a variety of designs throughout with green, black and white yarns and woven in black. There are short laces on both sides of the border. The three segments are then stitched together to make the shawl complete.

The Sangtam women are fond of red colour and thus most of their shawls are red. One of their most popular shawls is called '*Tsungrangshu*'. This shawl is also composed of three segments. The loom of the two outer segments are similarly made with three wide bands of black and red each with blue stripes here and there. The loom is woven in black. The middle segment is loomed with wide bands of black and red alternately. Red wool is fixed throughout along the successive bands. The loom is then woven in black. The three segments are stitched together to complete the shawl worn by the women. Their shawls are similar to that of the man's shawl of each tribe. They wear it on all important festivals and occasions.

A variety of colourful shawls are made and worn by the Konyak women. The most popular among them all is called Nyiko. This particular shawl is made up of four segments. The looms of the two outer segments are structured with white, red, blue and black. Thus, two middle segments are loomed with stripes of red, blue and black at the border but the major portion is made in white. It is woven in white putting various designs here and there along the stripes of red, blue and black. The four segments are now arranged properly and stitched together to complete it. There are laces on both ends of the shawl.

The Sema ladies too weave and wear a variety of colourful shawls. The most popular among them all is called *Chaktha Khumsi*. This particular shawl is composed of three segments and is normally four and a half feet in length. The loom of the middle segment is made up of three wide stripes of black. In between these black stripes a number of small bands in blue is sandwiched. The loom is woven in black while doing so, a number of horizontal designs in different colours are put in eight places. Again, in between these designs in the small blue stripes, a host of vertical designs are woven in nine places. The looms of the two outer segments are made, beginning with two small stripes of blue followed by five black band and four red bands successively. Black bands at both ends is wider than the other. On one end of the shawl colourful designs in eight places are put while the rest is being woven in black. The three segments will now be stitched together making a beautiful shawl to wear. There are laces on both ends of the shawl.

Lotukhwu is the original shawl of the Chakhesang women of Phek district. The loom is made with black threads and woven with the same short laces on both the ends. This shawl is completely black in colour like that of the Aos *"Angnaksü"*.

The ornaments and dresses used by various Naga tribes are too many to record in this piece of work. And to study and give a systematic account of all of them is beyond the scope of this book. That is why only some of the common ornaments and dresses used by majority of the Nagas have been recorded in this exercise.

Fig. 2.9A : The Women's Shawl

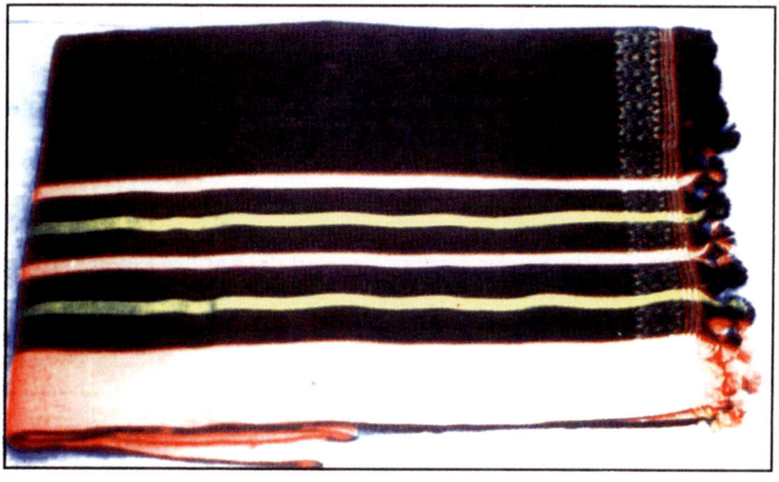

Fig. 2.9B : The Women's Shawl

Naga Attire And Musical Instruments
Naga Attire & Musical Instruments

3

THE NAGA MUSICAL INSTRUMENTS

By nature the Nagas are music lovers. Use of different musical instruments have been very common among the Nagas. They have been using different musical instruments for different purposes which are very interesting and recordable. In the past, boys and girls learned songs from their parents as well as from the elderly persons while sleeping in dormitory in groups (of course boys and girls separately). They learned many songs added with how to play various musical instruments as well. It was their system to communicate with each other through songs on many important matters either in group or in individual. For instance, if a man wanted to address and say something to a woman, he will rather speak through songs. This will again be replied through another appropriate song in response to him just as we find in Hindi film songs today. They used to argue and interact through songs in that manner. In this way they went on composing the words as well as the songs of deeper meaning. Thus, the traditional Naga songs are very philosophic. They used to sing various types of songs like the love songs, the song of appreciation and honour, the song in the field while working together. The vocal songs are usually accompanied by musical instruments especially on important occasions. The Naga traditional songs with musical accompaniment is beautiful and sweet to listen.

Unfortuantely, the youngsters are neglecting such traditional songs including the use of musical instruments. This part is highly regrettable. In this Chapter, some of the popular Naga musical instruments have been introduced.

3.1 The Bamboo Mouth-organ

The bamboo mouth-organ is one of the oldest traditional musical instruments used by the Nagas. This is a very simple instrument made of bamboo, yet very effective and enchanting. The making process of this musical instrument is not a very hard job. It neither requires hard labour nor heavy tools like *dao,* axe, etc. Among the musical instruments mouth-organ is the smallest one, yet, its uses are very important. Its whole length is about 6 inches long and half an inch in width. We canot use any kind of bamboo to make this instrument. *Ani*, a kind of thin bamboo is used to make this organ. Because, this quality of bamboo is found to be the best one for such instrument. In both the ends at least one inch should be left in such a way that it can be held putting the thumb and the pointing fingers. The other end is made like a nail head in which a string about eight inches long is tied for one and to pull it out separately. Throughout the length, a small portion of the centre is taken out vertically with the help of a sharp and pointed knife. The end where the fingers are holding is cut off so as to move the fingers easily. The other end remains uncut to block the air. This is called "Tongue". This tongue is taken out by means of a small pointed knife and thin out as round as a needle. The making process is then over and now completely ready to play. The end of the tongue portion should be placed between the lips and pull out the string or just beating the fingers at the end if one cannot use the string. This organ produces melodious sound. The Aos called it *Tepang Kongki.*

This musical instrument is not used in festivals, dances or other important occasions. It is played mostly inside the dormitory *Züki*; where young girls sleep. It can be played both by boys and girls too, without any restriction nor formal teaching is required to learn this small instrument. Players of this instrument can make four different sounds while playing. These four sounds are produced due to the movement of the fingers pulling the string, use of lips, breathing and the movement of the tongue by the player. The one who cannot play this instrument may not be able to identify these four different sounds. If a man wants to know these four different sounds, first of all, he must know how to play this instrument. This instrument is very simple, easy to make and play, but it takes a long time to become an expert of this organ.

Playing of this instrument by boys and girls indicate observance of secrecy of the lovers. For instance Mr. X wants to meet Miss. Y for some secrecy but in the presence of others, he is not in a postion to do anything freely. He has no other alternative way to convey her, therefore Mr. X plays the instrument saying that Miss Y is requested to come out for sometime to meet her lover. Miss. Y understands the meaning of the sound of the music taking lame excuses from the inmates, she comes out of the dormitory. Some time after, Mr. X follows her to meet outside for their secret affairs. Another example is that, while Miss Y plays this instrument saying that she is alone going to the field tomorrow and therefore Mr. X may follow her. Understanding the sound of the music, Mr. X follows her in the following day to enjoy their love affairs in the field. By nature, this type of music is played only at night when other people enjoy sound sleep. This music sound can be heard by all members who are living near by the area because its sound at night is very distinct. It is, therefore, known as the 'Midnight Musical Instrument', sounding midnight call.

This kind of musical instrument is used by all the Naga tribes calling different names. For example, in Ao dialect it is called *'Tebang Kongki'*. The same instrument is called *'Thekou'* by the Angamis and the Semas call it *'Aheu'*. The Zeliang people call it *'Kigong'*. The same is used by the Lothas and they call it *'Pyinggkhu'* or *'Khuking'*. Rengma tribe call it *'Atingo'* or *'Ken'*. The people of Konyak tribe call it *'Kongki'* and it is their favourite musical instrument. The Chang tribe also use this instrument by both boys and girls during the time of love making in dormitory. They call it *'Kongkhin'*. The people of Khiamngan use this instrument as their favourite one and they call it *'Ko-Kiang'*. Among the Phoms, this instrument is played by both boys and girls and they call it *'Phipe'*. The Yimchunger and Sangtams use the same instrument and they both call it *'Khongbi'*. In the district of Phek, Chakhesang people have been using this mouthorgan right from the beginning. Though it is a simple and small organ, it has been in use since times immemorial with great joy particularly for love making affairs in the olden days.

3.2 The Cup Violin

The Cup Violin is one of the musical instruments popularly used by the Aos. To make the Cup Violin, a good quality of hard and thin bamboo is selected or sometimes a shell of bittergourd is used. About 15 cm in length with a node in one end has to be finely cut out giving a shape of a cup or mug. A small hole is made 5 cm below the rim of the cup on both the sides of the cup opposite each other. Another piece of bamboo stick as thick as a finger and about two feet long is inserted through the holes made earlier and at least half an inch of the stick will be projecting out of the hole on the opposite sides. The artisan usually collects the hair from his lady lover since the instrument will be used in praise of her beauty. Neither knife nor *dao* is used to cut off the hair. Here, one can observe a deep emotional relationship between each other in the process of making this instrument as well as its uses. When the lovers are totally immersed in their passionate moment and the girl goes in a state of deep slumber, the boys baits a lock of hair from her nape without her knowledge. This lock of long human hair will be tied in the base of the bamboo rod and stretched over the bamboo to the other end and tied there. The mouth of the mug is covered by a dried outer covering of bamboo shoot. This covering is pressed in between the hair string and over the bamboo covering to make the string stronger.

Now, the cup violin is completely ready for use. Besides these, a bow is required to play. To make a bow, two things are important. Firstly, a thin bamboo half an inch in width and about a foot long is needed. Secondly, a bamboo fibre is thinned out with the help of the sharp *dao.* One end of this fibre will be tied in one end of the stick and the other end will be tied to the other end of the stick and it is cleaned by charcoal. Now, the bow is ready for use. Then one hand shall hold the long stick and the other end of the cup is put on the chest. The other hand shall hold the bow and rub on the hair string. By rubbing the hair string by the right hand and the left hand touching on the end hair string at different places produces the required musical tunes. According to tradition, it is said that hair of a talkative and promiscuous women is better for producing sharp sound and, therefore, such hair is used for making common violin.

As per the oral tradition, it is said that man learned the method of playing this instrument from the crab. When its ten fingers move one after another, it looks like the fingers of a pianoist playing piano. Out of this movement, men learned how to use his fingers while playing the violin, Both men and women can play this instrument without any restriction.

This cup violin made of hair is also played at night when everybody is asleep. On hearing the beautiful musical sound from a distance one remember his or her adolescent days and he becomes eager to know who the singer is. One might come across such a happy and contended free loving in one's life. This instrument is called Cup Violin or Mid Night Violin because it is played mainly at mid night.

The love of music and carefree life style is found to be very common among the Naga youths even today. The traditional musical instruments like bamboo mouthorgan and cup violin has been replaced by guitars and other electronic instruments today.

The Angamis and the Chakhesangs are fond of more merrymaking and dining in the dormitory. Their music is normally accompanied by a guitar type of instrument which is called a *'Tati'* and *'Lefu'* by the Chakhesangs. Like other tribes, the Semas also love music. Their singing is very melodious. Normally, they sing in responsory by two groups; a group of gents and another is female. They also use musical instrument of guitar type which is called *'Asuiku'*. Among the Konyak, they use a violin called *'Umo'*. Like Konyaks, the Zeliang tribe also use violin as they call it *'Kerabung'* Phom and Khiamngan tribes also use violin. They call it *'O-Khong'* and *'Poi-poi Thongthong'* respectively. It is really interesting and lovable to hear the sound of such tiny musical instruments at night.

3.3 The Bamboo Flute

The Naga flute is one of the most simple instruments made of thin bamboo. It produces beautiful sound with different tunes. Only a special quality of bamboo *'ani'* can be used to make such bamboo flute. This type of bamboo can make variety of musical intruments because it is much thinner than other type of bamboos with bigger holes in it; which can be used as musical instrument like *'Jemji'* or *'Penpa'* in Ao dialect. It is nothing but a flute which is commonly used in different parts of the world.

The process of making a flute is very simple, it does not require specific materials, tools and expert craftsmanship. A thin bamboo as big as a long roller used in the office is cut out without any knot at both the ends, one end of the bamboo is cut out in the shape of a nib. On the opposite side of the nib shape portion, a small hole is cut out with the help of a sharp knife. Again a small round nib shape wood is just pressed into the hole at the mouth of the nib shape portion. This round wood is provided with a small hole on it to make whistling sound when it is blown. Some four to six holes are to be pressed one after another vertically on it in the middle portion of the bamboo. These small holes are made for putting fingers blocking the air while playing. These are known as staff notation. The other main end remains as it is. All these works are done by an ordinary *dao* and it takes only about an hour, to manufacture a bamboo flute.

The bamboo flute is very easy to make and it has its own influence and pleasure on human psychology. There is no specific timing for blowing this flute but generally it is played after sunset. It is pleasurable to hear the music sound of a bamboo flute. For blowing the flute, it depends on individual expertise. It can be played by both men and women alike. Such musical instruments are mostly liked by boys and girls in particular; so, it is known as 'Youth instrument' and this is really an indigenous instrument used in a traditional way. To become a flutist one should undergo some formal training. It needs constant practice to become expertise in this instrument. One may take even years together to become master of this instrument.

This blowing instrument is used by every Naga tribe. The Angamis use this and they call it *'Lou'*. The Sema tribe also used this instrument and they call it *'Fulili'* in their dialect. Zeliang tribe also use the same instrument with great pleasure. They call it *'Nthiam'*. This instrument is used by Konyak tribe also and they named it *'Wewo'* in their dialect. Both the Aos and the Phoms had been using this flute from the very beginning. These two tribes call it as *'Jemji'*. The Lothas call it *'Philili'* and *'Kheli'* by the Rengmas. Like other tribes, the Khiamngans also use the same flute and it is known as *'Poipoi'* in their dialect. The Sangtams also use the same musical instrument mostly by boys and girls during their merry making. They call it *'Khongkoli'*.

Another type of musical instrument similar to this flute is called *'Malen'* in Ao dialect which is made out of paddy plant stump. Its making is again easier than that of a bamboo flute. Its whole length is nearly four to five inches only and as big as a lead pencil. It is made during harvest time only. To make it even *dao* or knife is not required but only a sickle. Even sometimes sickle is not required because sharp nail also could be used to make it. There is a knot in one of the ends, the other end is opened. Just near the knot, the stump may be broken by means of thumb and pointing finger. Three to four small holes are made on it to put fingers at the time of blowing. Hardly five minutes is required to make it into a blowing instrument. It does not last long because it dries up quickly. It can be used three to four hours only. It is often compared to a cicada which sings all day long and dies the next day. In the same way, this smallest of the flute is made just to sing some songs and broken for good. During harvest. time, girls return home carrying paddy from the field. They use to bring such flutes for blowing on the way for relief and happiness. Hearing the sound of such music enlightens them and they reach home at ease. The flute is played by all the Naga tribes but is not played during dancing and festival. Individually it is blown or played as per his wishes, yet it is seldom used during national festivals or on great occasions and dances. It is, therefore, regarded as most ordinary musical instrument.

3.4 The Trumpet

The trumpet is one of the oldest musical instruments used by different people of different countries for different purposes. This instrument is normally made of brass with a bright ringing tone. It makes a proclaiming loud sound once it is blown accurately. During the olden days it was used to proclaim the war signal especially by the Israelites during the time of Joshua, the Prophet. Even today the sound of a trumpet has significant meaning once it is blown, it indicates certain meanings. This musical instrument is also called the king of musical instruments of the world as the piano is regarded as the Queen of musical instruments.

Among the Nagas the use of trumpet was so common, though, it was not regarded as an important thing among the Nagas. Different types and shapes of trumpet are used by different tribes. For the purpose of making this trumpet, traditional materials like thin bamboo, buffalo horns, mithun horns, etc., were used. Whenever the Nagas slaugther such animals they always cut out the horns carefully with the help of an axe and *dao* and preserve it for making horn trumpet. Then the pointed end of the horn is cut off at least an inch so as to enable to make enough hole in it. The horn is then cleaned nicely with the best help of sharpening stone or sand. This small hole in the pointed horn is meant for putting the lips to blow it. The trumpet is also made by other materials like thin bamboo and cords. In case of a bamboo trumpet, a bamboo is cut as big as an arm about 4 to 5 feet with two nodes, one is in the upper and the other is in the centre or middle but the lower end is to be opened. A hole in the centre node is opened with the help of a spear blade to enable the sound to pass through the hole making the musical tone under the control of the tongue. Again, in the upper end of the node, a small hole is opened and another short bamboo pipe as big as a stick or a finger size has to be fixed tightly. This smaller pipe is to be put on the lips of the blower and thereby start blowing controlling the tongue and lips holding the bamboo trumpet with both the hands pressing towards the lips.

The Functions of the Trumpet

When the enemies attack the village, the sentry or the gate-keeper will immediately blow the trumpet so that the male members of the village will come out from their homes and assemble with war equipments and stand on battle footing. Again the warriors return home with their enemies heads, the message is first signalled through this trumpet. Most interestingly, when the village is on fire or when ferocious animals enter into the village, etc. the trumpeters will blow on the trumpet. It is also used in different merry making festival, worship etc., within the village by every Naga tribe. Again, those who do not use log drums, use this trumpet for giving information to the villagers. The people of Mon and Tuensang districts and the Ao people commonly use this trumpet but above all, the beating of log drum is more common and more important. In the sister State of Meghalaya, during the time of 'Kapamblang Nongrem' festival dance among the Khasis both men and women, boys and girls perform dance by blowing the trumpet. This national festival of the Khasis is very famous and attractive where they use such trumpet as one of the main items of their festival dance.

The use of trumpet is a major component in Naga culture. It carries lots of information. It is used in merry making during festival times, sometimes in accidents like fire in the village, attack of wild animals into the village, worship, etc. Therefore, it is just like the means of public address system used by the Department of Publicity and Information in present days. The trumpet which is made out of animal horns is called *'Kechu'*. The Aos consider this famous blowing instrument more important than other co-tribes. They use this instrument which is made of horn and thin bamboo. They called it *Jangzü* or *Tsüi.* The Zeliang tribe also use this instrument similar to that of the Angami type made out of animal horns and they call it *Mikia.* The Semas are very fond of animal rearing for instance, like mithun, buffalo, etc. Out of these horns they make the horn trumpet which is very popularly used for all occasions. They blow it in times of festival and in emergency as well. They call it *Afuko.* The people of Phek district use trumpet every now and then. It is their favourite and popular blowing instrument. They also make this trumpet with animal horns. Besides this, there is a kind of plant called *Thetsu.* It is neither a bamboo nor wood which is grown in the muddy places. It has enough holes inside the whole length though there are nodes in the plant. They also make trumpet out of this plant so they call it *Thetsu.* In Wokha district, the Lothas use this instrument with great pleasure. They use varieties of trumpet made out of different materials like animal horns and cords. It is used in merry making, national festival of the people and in times of emergency when threatened by enemies, wild animals and when the house is on

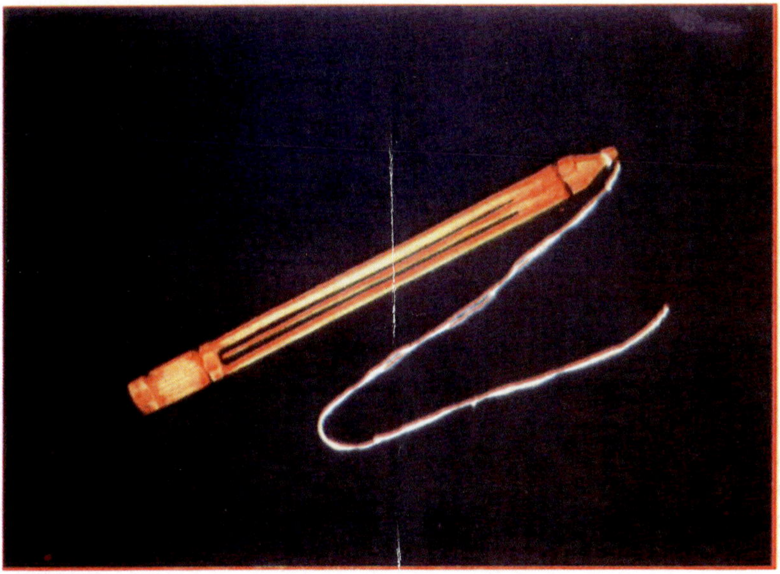

Fig. 3.1 : The Bamboo Mouth-organ

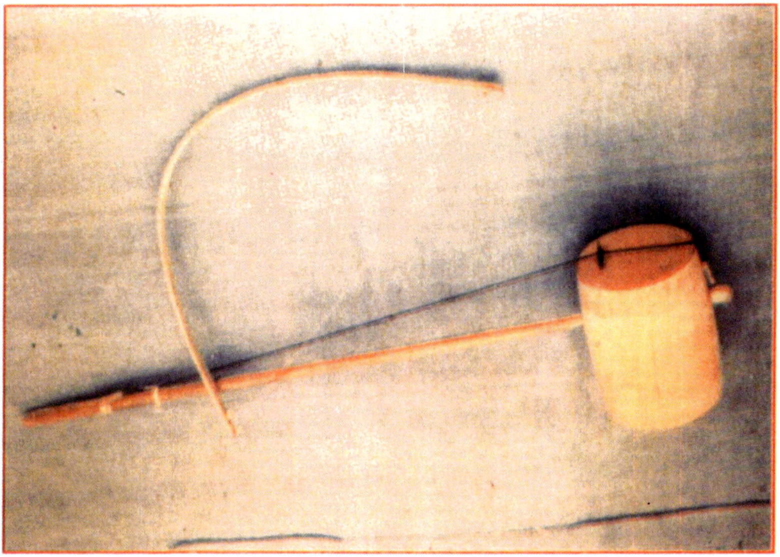

Fig. 3.2 : The Cup Violin

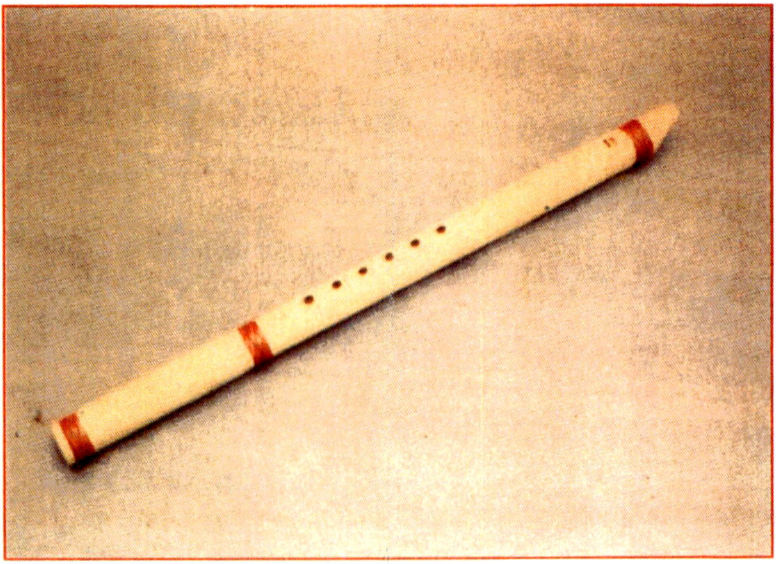

Fig. 3.3 : The Bamboo Flute

Fig. 3.4 : The Trumpet

fire, etc. They call it *Tatara.* Rengma Nagas use this trumpet as other tribes do. They also make this instrument with horns and bamboos. It is blown very often in the village indicating various meanings. They call it *Totitra.*

In Tuensang district too, some of the tribes use this trumpet for local and minor information within the village. Such blowing musical instruments are made out of animal horns. The Chang people call it *Teuklang.* The Phom tribe call it *Chekyong* and *Jangongmat* by Khiamngan. The Sangtam people call it as *Rudi.* For major information, the people of Tuensang district use log drum more popular than the trumpet in times of emergency. The Konyaks of Mon district use the same trumpet which is used by other tribes. The material used for making this instrument is mainly the animal horns. This instrument is called *'Nyaklong'* by the Konyaks. It is blown for sending messages to the people of that particular place in various ways. But for nationwide information, they beat the log drum as in case of Tuensang tribes of Nagaland.

3.5 The Drum

Of all the musical instruments, the drum is one of the most popular instruments used by almost all the people of all countries. Such musical instruments are of different kinds and shapes; some are big and some are small. Of the musical instruments, the bamboo mouthorgan is the smallest and the drum is the biggest. The songs sung during Naga festival and dance without beating a drum, sounds so dull and monotonous. That is why, the drum is considered as the leading instrument.

India is a land of rich culture and the use of drum is found to be so popular. There are different kinds of drums with different shapes and sizes according to the cultural background of the people. The drum is used in different places for different purposes. For instance, the Garo people of Meghalaya State use a longer shape about four to five feet in length but its circumference is about two feet and some inches only. The Rajasthani drums are very big and round in shape. It requires at least five to six men to carry it. Thus the Rajasthani drum is considered to be the biggest drum in India. It is kept on the ground, and ten persons will beat it at a time. In Karnataka State, there is a dance known as *"Drum Dance".* During the occasion of Inter State Cultural Programme of India and other important functions, the expert drummers exhibit such socio-cultural dances beating such giant drums.

It makes the national festival of India so rich.

In every month, except June, tribes of Nagaland observe their national festivals. Among the Aos, there are two festivals *Moastü* and *Tsüngrem Mong*. They are observed in the first week of May and August respectively of every year. *Miu* and *Tsoküm* festivals are observed by the people of Khiamngan of Tuensang district in different months every year. All Naga tribes are festival and dance lovers. They observe the tribal festivals with dances and beating the drum.

Process of Making Drum

First of all, a seasoned or dried wood is cut off at least about two feet long with its circumference about two and half feet. Both the ends are made little smaller than the middle portion and therefore it becomes an oval shape. After this, a thorough hole is made as big as possible enabling to produce enough musical sound. The two big mouths or holes of the drum is then covered by cow's skin which is purposefully arranged for this instrument. The leather or cow skin is then put round the holes tightly and stitched with the cane fibre carefully. It becomes very hard when the skin is dried. And thereby the drum become lighter and ready to be used. To make it more beautiful and handy, the cover of the drum is nicely knitted by the cane fibre round the body of the drum. Again, a cane belt is tied up from right to left, to enable to carry the drum conveniently on the shoulder of the drummer. The Naga people keep at least two or three drums in every village. But in the bigger villages one will find even more than three or four drums in every *khel.*

According to tradition, the drum is made by the concerned *Khel* people only. It is made in the premises of the Morung house normally. And it is kept in the house of a responsible man of the *khel* or in the Morung itself.

The functions of a drum are manifold. Firstly, the sound of the drum controls the uniform movement of the dancers, hence this drum is regarded as the dancer's guide. Secondly, when a responsible leader of the *khel* or village dies, at that time, the drum is beaten to show respect and honour to the departed soul. This particular beating of drum on such occasion is called *'Jepjongpen'* in Ao dialect which means mourning beating. Thirdly, the beating of the drum is associated with the appearances of lunar and solar eclipse. There is a superstition among the Nagas that the Moon and the Sun are sometimes eaten by a huge tiger, and so the Nagas especially the Aos of Mokokchung district mourn on such occasion by beating the drum, praying to Lichaba, the Creator of heaven and Earth to save the Moon and the Sun.

In Zeliang society also, the drum is used for similar purposes as that of the Ao tribe. There is a dance known as 'Hornbill Dance of the Zeliangs. In this dance, there are two opposite rows of boys and girls. Each and every dancer use to have one Hornbill tail in his or her hand. Again, there is a bigger group of people standing near the area where they perform the dance. Now, along with the beating of drum by the music party or group, the dancers move their legs and bodies in uniform. According to the rhythm of the beating of drum, boys and girls start dancing. For the people of Zeliang tribe there is a national day known as *'Nga-Ngai'*. In this festival, people enjoy maximum happiness with their best traditional dresses. This is the famous festival of Zeliang tribe. In such occasion the drummer starts to beat the drum creating emotion of the merry making people. This musical instrument is called '*Chum*' in Zeliang dialect.

3.6 The Naga Log Drum

According to tradition, once upon a time, it is believed that the Nagas were living near an ocean. It is said that they lived elsewhere in South East Asia surrounded by the oceans. There are many logical reasons on this matter though there is no authentic record. The Nagas moved from place to place in search of a better place for living. They travelled for many years from one place to another across Thailand, China, Central Asia and reached the present Myanmar from where they landed into the present abode. Our forefathers had wisely chosen to settle on the hill tops to save themselves from the enemy's attacks. They made boats or rafts with bamboos and crossed over the big rivers on their journey. Though they went farther from the ocean, the ships and boats in their memory became a legend to them. In order to preserve this sweet memory they made objects like drums by huge trees. They kept this in their villages. This is one of the biggest drum used by the Nagas. Since it was never moved out of the same place, and it looked very particular; out of curiosity perhaps they hit it with sticks or stones which gave sound like tong....tong..., kong..kong. It is because of this peculiar sound, it was named 'Tongten' or 'Süngkong' and people call it by that name even today. Tongten or Süngkong is an Ao name which denotes the sound of the drum, the long drum which gives a loud and distinctive sound.

The log drum is not used by all the Naga tribes. It is seen popularly among the Aos, the Konyaks, the Sangtams, the Phoms, the Changs and the Khiamngan and the Yimchungers. Thus, one will find at least one or two such drums in every village of these tribes.

The size of the log drum varies from place to place and from village to village. In a small village there is only one log drum which may be smaller in size but in bigger villages, each *khel* or sector has one log drum and is bigger in size too. In every *khel* or sector they also make one dormitory, *Arju,* in Ao dialect and kept one log drum each in every *Arju* of that village. The *Morung* or *Arju* plays a major role in making a log drum. However, in small villages, where the male members are less, all the adult male members gather and decide to make a log drum and work together. In both the cases, a witch or wizard is consulted first and following his/her direction the place and type of the tree is selected. After consultation with the witchcraft or witch doctor, only a few people are selected to cut the wood first. Only after that, the remaining people could work turn by turn in the process of making the log drum following taboos strictly:

The Process of Making

1. The first step is the selection of a good log at least about 38 ft long, 13 to 14 ft girth and its tail 5 to 6 ft. The circumference of the drum depends upon the size of the tree. The trunk of the tree i.e., the log drum is divided into three major parts namely the head, the body and the tail.
2. The expert artisans are then engaged in designing the head portion. Because it is the most difficult task of the artisans needing careful decision. The head of the log drum is to be made like a boat's shape with a human face at one end of the log.
3. There is a special task force who engage in blacksmithy work for repairing of *daos,* axe, hoes, etc. They supply required tools and implements to the workers.
4. The body of the log drum is laboriously hollowed out through a long slite about a foot wide running down the length of the drum. The bigger the hole, the clearer and louder the sound would be.
5. The adult male members of the *khel* or sector in the village do all the physical works, while the womenfolk prepare food and drink for the men who are engaged in heavy work. The younger male members supply food and drink to the workers. This

division of work is followed till the log drum is finished. Then the route is cut straight for pulling the drum. Round and strong trees cut to be used as rollers over which the drum is pulled. These works are done by male members.

6. The last step involves in making of such drum is painting of the head of the log drum. For this purpose two colours are required. Charcoal is used for black and blood of the pig and fowl is used for red colour.
7. All the workers are engaged in different tasks. They stay in the jungle till the work is finally completed. When the carving and making of its body is over, many strong ropes and wild creepers are tied ceremoniously from head to tail for pulling the log. Then a day is appointed with great feasting and prayer for pulling the log drum. The drum pulling ceremony is one of the greatest ceremonies. During its pulling such songs are sung:

Oh! yongpang süngdi;
Lima nakba süngko,
Yimkongwapang chang,
Aren henba, nang penlir, zongzar;
Nang mongjen nü aset angni.

English version:
Oh! the source of stream,
Huge tree of jungle guardian,
The umberlla of the forest,
Carrier of blessing to the villagers,
Your hear-trobs longingly awaits,
To you original place, step ahead.

Both men and women put on their traditional dresses and they sing, dance and shout; while pulling the long drum together. It looks like a multitude of ants carrying a death earthworm to their home for food. To maintain balance of pulling, they put matted posts in the hole and over these posts, some selected elderly persons sit to control the movement of the drum. While dragging the drum they lay the wooden rollers about 6 to 7 ft. horizontally throughout the route and move over it easily and the same is carried by the male members till the log drum reaches the place where it has to be kept.

On reaching the village, it is kept in a sacred place normally in front of the dormitory; and a shed is constructed to protect it. Some 20 to 30 pieces of strikers about 2 feet long are made to beat the drum. They are kept inside the hollow when not in use. Two more strikers like posts are tied in both sides of posts or pillars of the shed and they are placed on the log drum in a slanting position. These two strikers are used to produce louder sound and the smaller ones are used for softer sound at the same time producing different sounds and meanings.

The Aos worship this drum with fresh heads. In such a worship animal blood or human blood was sacrificed alongwith feasting and drinking. In olden days, any stranger, either friend or foe who unfortunately came to the village on that particular day, when a new drum was dragged, was killed. His head was the first to be put on the drum. But at present, this log drum is not worshipped anymore as before. Now-a-days, it is made just to keep as a tourist attraction and only as a legendary model. The log drum has become a mere souvenire of the past.

Functions of the Log Drum

The functions of the log drum are various:

(i) It gives information for a public meeting giving a clarion call.
(ii) It gives message to the villagers by beating the drum when the village is on fire.
(iii) When the village is attacked by the enemies, the drum is beaten making a peculiar sound about the situation.
(iv) When the warriors return home with their trophy (head) the message is proclaimed by beating the drum.
(v) It is also used when a tiger or a wild bear is being chased.
(vi) During Lunar and Solar Eclipse, they beat the drum and mourn for the sun to rise again.
(vii) It protects, guides and blesses its worshippers. That is why it is called the village deity also.

There is a variety of difference in the style of beating the drum producing different sounds indicating different meanings or messages. The messages of the drum may differ from village to village, therefore, secrecy could be passed on without any difficulty. That is why, this log drum plays a very significant role in Naga society. In the olden days they used to worship the log drum with animal's blood; sometimes with human blood also. But today, such practices are no more available. Thus, this log drum will be found of souvenir in Naga villages as a sample.

In many villages log drums are not found today. The Konyak Nagas call it *Shum*. All the five tribes in Tuensang district use log drum. In every village of these five tribes has at least one or more log drums till today. The Khiamngan Nigas called it *Phean*; and the Changs call it *Tongsen* whereas the Sangtams call it *Singkong*. The Hukphang village of Phom tribe is a big one. In this village, each *khel* has one log drum respectively. They call it *Thongh*. The Yimchungers call it *Sangkong*.

Thus, the use of log drum is found to be a common practice among the Naga tribes. Many original log drums were burnt by fire when the Naga villages were forcibly burnt by the Indian forces during 1950s to 1960s throughout Nagaland. Also, most of the original ornaments and dresses were burnt into ashes during that period. In many villages there were three to four log drums; but all were destroyed by fire during those days.

The Nokpu villagers of Ao tribe are very talented in making handicrafts. They have special talent and can carve stones and woods very beautifully. There is an interesting story about this village in making a log drum. It is said that once upon a time, the Nokpu villagers cut a big tree to make a beautiful log drum they ever made. After finishing it they tried to pull it to the village but it did not move at all. However, on consulting a witch doctor, they were told that the wife of the *Arju Jozen* must join the pulling ceremony. Because she was not in the crowd when they tried to pull the drum. She was not there because she was pregnant at that time. As requested by the village elders she decided to participate in the pulling ceremony. The villagers were excited to see her but the nature began to mourn over the life of a young woman whose end was drawing nearer. The day suddenly became dark and started raining showing its unhappiness. It was said that this young woman was a very good singer too. She was aware of her death, yet with cheerful face, she sang a song to the log drum and pulled the rope that was tied to it. Soon, it rolled in full speed and she was crashed beneath it.

This is the song sang by her, her mother and her husband. (English version)

Mighty tree of stream;
Thou art from childhood;
Beyond the Riong River;
Growth for me.

This morn, Nokpu Atu belles;
Worn long white clothes;
Coming for thee looking
Run, mighty log drum.

Men of Nokpu Atu bucks;
Who said to worhsip this mighty;
My beloved bride of the street;
Rise up from her death.

Mother of beloved wife;
Don't weep, brave warriors;
Stone over the coronet;
Put like horn-bill tail.

Fig. 3.5 : The Drum

Fig. 3.6 : The Naga Log Drum

INDEX